SELLING OPTIONS FOR INCOME

FOR INCOME

A COMPLETE GUIDE TO THE WHEEL

STRATEGY AND BUILDING

FINANCIAL FREEDOM

ONE PREMIUM AT A TIME

TONY PEREZ

DRAGON
PUBLISHING

Disclaimer

This book is provided for educational and informational purposes only and does not constitute financial, investment, legal, or tax advice. The material presented reflects the author's personal opinions and trading experiences and should not be interpreted as a recommendation to buy, sell, or hold any security or financial instrument.

Trading options involves substantial risk and may not be suitable for all investors. Readers should carefully consider their financial situation and consult a qualified financial professional before making any investment decisions.

Past performance does not guarantee future results. All examples are provided for illustrative purposes only. The author assumes no responsibility for any financial losses or damages resulting from the use or misuse of the information contained in this book.

Examples of trades, positions, or strategies discussed are not recommendations and are intended solely to demonstrate concepts related to risk management, defensive trading, and income strategy execution.

TABLE OF CONTENTS

THE OPTIONS INCOME SERIES BY TONY PEREZ

The Options Income Series is a practical, experience-driven guide for traders who want to generate consistent income through option selling while managing risk across all market conditions.

Rather than chasing predictions, hype, or short-term market moves, this series focuses on probability, discipline, and repeatable systems that treat trading like a business.

Each volume builds on the last while remaining fully stand-alone.

Volume I focuses on the foundations of income-based options trading, including the Wheel Strategy, cash-secured puts, covered calls, and disciplined position management.

Future volumes address capital preservation, recovery strategies, and long-term survival during volatile and declining markets.

This series is written for traders who value consistency over excitement, structure over speculation, and long-term durability over short-term thrills.

INTRODUCTION

When I first started learning about options, it seemed complicated: Greeks, deltas, strike prices, probabilities. I almost quit before I began. But once I realized that options aren't about predicting where a stock will go—they're about managing time, probability, and emotion—everything changed.

This book isn't about chasing huge wins. It's about building steady, repeatable income, created one premium at a time. And the best part is that you don't need to guess the market's direction to win.

The truth is simple: If you can stay patient, follow a system, and sell options on great stocks at great prices, the market will pay you consistently.

In these pages, you'll learn exactly how to do that. No jargon. No complicated formulas. No theory for the sake of theory.

Just clear, simple, practical strategies that ordinary traders use every day to generate real income, especially using the Wheel Strategy—the method at the heart of this book.

By the time you finish, you will understand how to:

- Identify the best stocks for option selling
- Use cash-secured puts and covered calls to bring in weekly or monthly income
- Build and manage positions the smart way
- Roll losing trades into winning ones
- Think like a professional option seller, not a gambler
- Grow your account over time through consistency and discipline

My goal is for you to say, "I get it, and I can actually do this."

Who This Book Is *Not* For

This book is intentionally not for readers who:

- Are looking for overnight riches
- Want "lottery ticket" trades
- Chase adrenaline, excitement, or hype
- Believe the market owes them quick profits
- Prefer guessing over discipline
- Want to trade earnings, memes, or rumors
- Expect every week to be a winner
- Are unwilling to follow rules or manage risk

If you're searching for shortcuts, thrill trades, or instant wealth, this book will likely disappoint you.

This book is for readers who:

- Want consistent, repeatable income
- Value probability over prediction
- Understand that patience is a skill
- Are willing to follow a system
- Prefer boring consistency over emotional swings
- Want to lower risk while generating income
- Treat trading like a business, not a gamble
- Are comfortable letting time and discipline do the work

The Wheel Strategy is not exciting, and that's precisely why it works.

If you commit to consistency, structure, and discipline, the methods in this book can help you build a reliable income stream over time.

If you don't, no strategy will save you.

Read on with clarity, patience, and realistic expectations, and you'll get exactly what this book promises.

How to Use the Info Nuggets

Throughout this book, you'll notice special highlighted sections called Info Nuggets. These Nuggets exist for one purpose, to give you the exact insights, warnings, shortcuts, and real-world wisdom that professional option sellers use every day.

While the main text teaches you the strategy, the Nuggets teach you the judgment—the part most traders never learn until they've made expensive mistakes.

Each Nugget delivers one or more of the following:

- Practical guidance

- Risk warnings

- Probability advantages

- Pro tips used by professionals

- Common mistakes to avoid

- Smarter ways to manage trades

In other words, the Nuggets are your built-in mentor. They're placed exactly where a real mentor would stop you and say, "Pay attention. This part matters."

You *can* skim the book without reading the Nuggets, but you'll become a far more confident and profitable trader if you read them carefully.

As you move through the chapters, treat each Nugget as:

- A checkpoint

- A strategic reminder

- A shortcut to better decisions

- A reinforcement of professional trading mindset

These Nuggets alone can save you months of learning and thousands of dollars in avoidable mistakes. Use them. Review them. Come back to them often.

If you ever feel uncertain about a trade, reread the Nuggets. They often contain the exact decision rule you need.

Welcome to *Selling Options for Income*.

Let's build your financial freedom, one premium at a time.

AUTHOR'S NOTE

I wrote this book after years of real-world trading experience—not in classrooms or institutions but through self-study, discipline, and thousands of hours of practical work.

Like many traders, I started by reading every book I could find. But most of them were filled with fluff, unnecessary complexity, or theory that didn't actually help you place better trades. I wanted something different.

So, I created the book I *wished I had when I started*—clear, simple, actionable, and focused only on what truly matters.

No fluff.

No confusion.

Just proven strategies explained the way real traders use them.

I built this for you, the everyday trader who wants financial freedom, steady income, and a system that actually works.

This book focuses on generating options income under normal market conditions. Extended drawdowns and recovery-focused strategies are addressed in later volumes of this series.

Tony Perez

Part I

FOUNDATIONS

CHAPTER 1

WHY TRADE OPTIONS

Most people think options are risky, complicated, or reserved for elite traders. In reality, when used correctly, especially as an options seller, not a buyer, options can be one of the most stable, repeatable income tools available to everyday investors.

Options selling is considered so safe by many brokerage firms that they even allow you to do it inside retirement accounts—including Roth IRAs.

Brokerages do *not* permit high-risk strategies or margin trading in IRAs, yet they still allow:

- Cash-secured puts
- Covered calls

Why? Because these strategies have defined risk, are backed by cash or shares, and align with the conservative nature of long-term retirement planning. If a strategy is safe enough for a Roth IRA, it's safe enough to be a foundation for steady, repeatable income.

This chapter lays the foundation for why you should consider using options, how they create reliable income, and why professional traders rely on the same principles you're about to learn.

1. Options Give You More Control

When you trade stocks, you have two choices:

- Buy shares
- Sell shares

That's it.

But with options, you have more control:

- You choose your price
- You choose your time frame
- You choose your income level
- You choose your probability of success

Instead of chasing stocks at unpredictable prices, you let the market come to you, and get paid while you wait.

This is why selling options (especially cash-secured puts and covered calls) is such a powerful strategy for income-focused traders.

2. Options Can Generate Income Even When the Stock Doesn't Move

With option selling, your profit doesn't depend on the stock going up.

You can make money when a stock:

- Goes up
- Stays flat
- Even drops a little

That's the beauty of premium selling; time decay works in your favor.

Nugget: The Probability Advantage

When you sell an option with a 20 delta, you're starting the trade with approximately an 80% probability of success.

No traditional stock strategy gives you odds that strong before the trade even begins.

3. Selling Options Can Reduce Risk Compared to Stock-Only Investing

Most people don't realize this, but selling certain types of options actually reduces risk.

For example:

- If you sell a cash-secured put, you're agreeing to buy a stock you already want at a discount, while getting paid.
- If you sell a covered call, you're collecting premium on shares you already own.

In both cases, you are paid to wait.

This is one of the few investing strategies where time and probability are on your side, instead of fighting against you.

Nugget: Why Pros Sell, Not Buy

Professional traders, hedge funds, and market makers are overwhelmingly net sellers of options.

They rely on:

- time decay (theta)
- controllable risk
- and consistent income

Retail traders lose money because they *buy* options.

Professionals make money because they *sell* them.

4. Options Allow You to Set Your Own Paycheck

Every time you sell an option, someone pays you a premium upfront.

That premium:

- Is yours immediately
- Is not refundable
- Can be repeated weekly or monthly
- Works like a self-created paycheck

For example, selling a put for $2.00 ($200 per contract) means you receive $200 instantly, even if the stock goes nowhere.

Nugget: Get Paid to Wait

Selling cash-secured puts is the only strategy where you:

- Get paid upfront
- To *possibly* buy a stock you already want
- At a discount you choose

It's the closest thing in the market to naming your own purchase price—and getting paid while your order waits.

5. Options Allow You to Profit from Time Decay (Theta)

One of the biggest advantages option sellers have is theta decay.

Time decay works like this:

- Every day that passes, an option loses value.
- Sellers want the option to lose value.
- Buyers fight against time.
- Sellers profit because of time.

This means you no longer need perfect timing—you just need patience.

6. Options Let You Build a Consistent Income System

When you combine:

- Cash-secured puts
- Covered calls
- Rolling strategies
- Good stock selection

You get something powerful:

A repeatable income machine.

This book will show you how to build a system that:

- Targets weekly or monthly revenue
- Reduces risk through careful selection
- Generates predictable income
- Keeps emotions out of trading

Your goal is consistency, not excitement.

In This Chapter, You Learned:

- Options can be safer when sold strategically
- Premium income can repeat weekly
- You control the strike, timeframe, and risk
- You can profit even when stocks don't move
- Time decay works for sellers, not buyers
- Options selling forms the foundation of a consistent income system

CHAPTER 2

THE LANGUAGE OF OPTIONS

When you first start learning options, the terminology can feel overwhelming. The good news is this: you only need a small set of core terms to understand how to sell options successfully.

By the end of this chapter, you will be fluent in the language of option selling, and everything else in the book will click into place.

1. The Option Contract

An option contract controls 100 shares of a stock.

That means:

- 1 contract = 100 shares

- 2 contracts = 200 shares

- 5 contracts = 500 shares

When you see a premium of $1.25, that really means $1.25 × 100 = $125 received (or paid, if you're buying instead of selling, which we rarely do).

Nugget: Why 100 Shares Matters

Options were designed around 100-share blocks because institutions trade in round lots.

For sellers, this creates predictable income math—every $1.00 in premium is always $100 cash received.

2. Calls vs. Puts

Call Option

A call option gives someone the right to buy shares from you at a certain price.

When you sell a call:

- You are agreeing to sell your shares at the strike price if assigned.
- You collect a premium for making that agreement.

This is the foundation of the covered call.

Put Option

A put option gives someone the right to sell shares to you at a certain price.

When you sell a put:

- You are agreeing to buy shares at the strike price if assigned.
- You collect a premium for making that agreement.

This is the basis of the cash-secured put.

Nugget: The Only Two Agreements You Need to Know

Every option contract—no matter how complicated it seems—boils down to just two agreements:

- "I'll buy shares at this price if needed."
- "I'll sell shares at this price if needed."

Once you understand those two, you understand 90% of the entire options market.

3. Strike Price

This is the price at which the option can be exercised.

Examples:

- Sell a \$20 put → you agree to buy shares at \$20.
- Sell a \$25 call → you agree to sell shares at \$25.

You choose the strike price: meaning you control the deal.

4. Expiration Date

All options expire on a certain day.

Common expirations:

- Weekly (every Friday)
- Monthly (3rd Friday of the month)

As sellers, we choose how long we want to hold the trade:

- 7 days
- 14 days
- 30–45 days

Time decay (theta) works in your favor more quickly with shorter expirations.

Nugget: Why Shorter Dates Pay You Faster

Theta accelerates as expiration gets closer.

This means a 7-day option might lose value 4x faster than a 30-day option.

Faster decay = faster income for sellers.

5. Premium

Premium = the amount you receive upfront for selling the option.

Example:

- Sell a contract for \$2.00 premium → you receive \$200
- Sell for \$0.85 → you receive \$85

You keep this premium no matter what happens next.

6. ITM, ATM, OTM

These describe where the option is relative to the current stock price.

OTM – Out of the Money (where we usually sell)

- A put is OTM when the strike is below the stock price.
- A call is OTM when the strike is above the stock price.

OTM options are safer for income.

ATM – At the Money

- The strike is roughly the same as the stock price.
- Riskier, but higher premium.

ITM – In the Money

- A put is ITM when the strike is above the stock price.
- A call is ITM when the strike is below the stock price.

ITM options have higher risk and higher premium, not recommended for Wheel beginners.

7. The Greeks (Simple Version)

You don't need to know all the Greeks deeply, just two of them:

Delta

Delta measures probability.

Rule of thumb:

- Delta 0.30 ≈ 70% probability of profit
- Delta 0.20 ≈ 80% probability of profit
- Delta 0.10 ≈ 90+% probability of profit

We will use delta strategically in later chapters.

Nugget: Delta Is Your Probability Engine

Forget complicated math—delta is just a probability dial.

Lower delta = higher chance of success.

You control your own win rate before the trade even begins.

Theta (Time Decay)

Theta tells you how much value the option loses each day.

And since you are the seller, time decay makes the option worth less, benefiting you.

8. Assignment

Assignment happens when the buyer chooses to exercise the option.

If you sold a put:

- Assignment → you buy 100 shares at the strike price.

If you sold a call:

- Assignment → you sell 100 shares at the strike price.

Assignment is not a bad thing—it is a normal part of the Wheel Strategy.

In This Chapter, You Learned:

- Calls = right to buy | Puts = right to sell
- One contract = 100 shares
- Premium = income
- Strike price = your chosen price
- Expiration dates determine time decay
- OTM is safest for income selling
- Delta gives probability of profit
- Assignment is expected (not scary)

CHAPTER 3

HOW OPTIONS ARE PRICED

To sell options for income, you don't need to predict the future, but you do need to understand why an option is worth what it's worth.

Option pricing might seem complicated, but in reality, there are only a few key forces that matter to us as sellers.

This chapter breaks them down in simple, everyday language.

1. The Three Main Forces That Create Option Prices

Option prices are primarily driven by:

1. Stock Price
2. Time Remaining Until Expiration
3. Volatility (IV)

Everything else is just math behind the scenes.

Let's break these down.

Nugget: You Don't Need the Math

Wall Street uses complex equations to price options, but the Wheel trader only needs three questions:

- Where is the stock price?
- How much time is left?
- How volatile is the stock right now?
- Master those three, and you understand 90% of pricing.

2. How Stock Price Affects Option Value

When the stock price moves closer to the strike price, the option becomes more valuable.

For Puts:

- If the stock drops, the put becomes more valuable (bad for you as the seller).
- If the stock rises or stays flat, the put loses value (good for you).

For Calls:

- If the stock rises, the call becomes more valuable (bad for you).
- If the stock stays flat or drops, the call loses value (good for you).

As sellers, we profit when the option becomes worthless over time.

Nugget: Price Moves Fast, Premium Moves Faster

An option's value can change faster than the stock price because pricing reflects probability.

If the market thinks something *might* happen, the premium jumps instantly—even if the stock hasn't moved yet.

3. Time Decay (Theta): The Seller's Best Friend

Time decay is the most important force in options selling.

Here's the simple truth:

- Every single day, the option loses value because it is closer to expiration.
- Buyers are fighting against the clock.
- Sellers (you) are benefiting from the clock.

Theta decay accelerates in the final 30 days, which is why many Wheel traders focus on:

- 7–10 day expirations (weeklies)
- 14–16 day expirations
- 30–45 day expirations

Shorter expirations = faster decay = faster income.

Nugget: Theta Speeds Up, Never Slows Down

Theta decay is not linear—it accelerates. That's why a 7-day option may lose value five times faster than a 45-day option.

Faster decay = more opportunities for consistent income.

4. Implied Volatility (IV)

IV is how much the market expects the stock to move.

High IV = higher option premiums

Low IV = lower option premiums

Examples:

- Earnings week → IV spikes → premiums increase
- Calm markets → IV falls → premiums shrink

As an income seller, higher IV is usually good as long as the stock is solid.

Nugget: IV Measures Fear and Uncertainty

High IV doesn't mean a stock *will* move—it means traders *fear* it might.

Sellers get paid more during fear because buyers pay extra for protection or speculation.

5. Why the Black-Scholes Model Doesn't Matter to You

Most option pricing is based on math models like Black-Scholes. You do *not* need to know that formula.

You only need to understand:

- Options become cheaper as time passes
- Options become cheaper if volatility drops
- Options become cheaper when they move OTM

That's it.

6. Intrinsic Value vs. Extrinsic Value

Options are made of two components:

Intrinsic Value

- The amount the option is ITM.

Example:

If a $20 call has a stock price of $22, intrinsic value = $2.00.

Extrinsic Value

- Time value + volatility value.

Example:

If the same call is trading at $2.50, then:

- Intrinsic = 2.00
- Extrinsic = 0.50

As sellers, we aim to sell options with high extrinsic value because that's the part that evaporates with time.

Nugget: Extrinsic = The Seller's Paycheck

Intrinsic value is real, immediate value.

Extrinsic value is the part you get paid for—and the part that disappears daily.

That's why sellers target OTM options: they are almost pure extrinsic value.

7. Why Extrinsic Value Makes You Money

Extrinsic value shrinks every day. Buyers lose. Sellers win.

The more extrinsic value an option has:

- The more you collect
- The faster it decays
- The sooner you profit

This is why OTM options are so attractive—they're almost all extrinsic value.

In This Chapter, You Learned:

- Options are priced based on stock price, time, and volatility
- Time decay works for you
- Higher IV = higher premium
- Intrinsic value is real value; extrinsic is time value
- You profit when extrinsic value disappears

CHAPTER 4

RISK AND REWARD

Before you ever place a single options trade, you need to understand one thing clearly:

Options selling is powerful, but only if you respect risk.

This chapter shows you how to think about risk and reward the way professional income traders do: calmly, logically, and with a system.

1. All Trading Has Risk, But You Can Choose Your Level

Stock-only traders have limited control:

- Buy and hope it goes up
- Sell and hope it was the right time

Options sellers have more control because you can choose:

- Your strike price
- Your probability of profit
- Your timeframe
- Your income level
- Your risk tolerance

In other words…

You choose your risk before entering the trade.

That alone separates professional traders from emotional gamblers.

Nugget: Risk Isn't the Enemy—Uncertainty Is

The goal of options selling isn't to eliminate risk (that's impossible).

It's to define risk so clearly that nothing surprises you.

When risk is known and controlled, trading becomes a business—not a guess.

2. The Wheel Strategy Reduces Risk by Design

The Wheel Strategy works in this sequence:

1. Sell a cash-secured put
2. If assigned, you own 100 shares
3. Then you sell a covered call on those shares
4. Repeat

Why is this lower risk?

- You always choose a stock you're comfortable owning
- You choose a strike price below market value
- You collect income whether assigned or not
- You reduce your cost basis with every premium collected

Assignment is not a failure—it is part of the plan.

Nugget: Premium Reduces Risk Automatically

Every premium you collect lowers your cost basis.

A lower cost basis means:

- Less downside risk
- Faster break-even
- Higher long-term returns

This is why the Wheel is considered one of the safest income strategies available.

3. How to Think About Max Loss (The Right Way)

Most beginners obsess over max loss numbers shown by brokers.

Let's simplify:

- Cash-Secured Put max loss = if the company goes bankrupt
- Covered Call max loss = same as owning the stock normally

But here's the key difference:

Selling premium lowers your cost basis, and therefore lowers your risk, every week.

As long as you choose strong companies and sensible strikes, the Wheel becomes one of the most durable strategies available.

Nugget: Max Loss Numbers Are Theoretical, Not Realistic

Broker platforms calculate max loss assuming the stock goes to zero overnight.

That rarely happens.

Real risk is reduced dramatically by:

- choosing quality stocks
- selling OTM strikes
- collecting premium consistently

Don't fear the theoretical—manage the practical.

4. The Most Common Risk: Emotional Trading

The biggest risk in options selling isn't the market.

It isn't volatility.

It isn't assignment.

It's this:

Breaking your own rules.

Examples of emotional mistakes:

- Selling too close to the money for a bigger premium

- Trading on bad stocks because the IV is high
- Rolling too late
- Not taking profits at 50%
- Position sizes that are too big

The market doesn't punish patience.

It punishes impulse.

Nugget: The Market Rewards Discipline

Consistent traders don't win because they're smarter.

They win because they:

- trade small
- stay mechanical
- avoid impulsive decisions
- follow the plan no matter what

Your system saves you from yourself.

5. Your Risk Is Determined Before You Click Sell

Professional sellers do this before every trade:

1. Choose a stock you're willing to own
2. Pick a strike with the right delta (usually 0.20–0.30)
3. Check the chart and IV
4. Size the trade properly
5. Plan your exit before entering

If you do these steps, your risk is controlled from the start.

6. Small Premiums, Big Safety

You might see a put offering $15 or $20 and think, *That's not worth it.*

Professional sellers think differently:

- Small premiums = low risk
- High premiums = high risk
- Consistency beats excitement

Your income grows over time through repetition, not from taking oversized trades.

7. Reward Comes from Systems, Not Predictions

You don't need to guess earnings.

You don't need to predict news.

You don't need to know where the market will go next month.

Your income comes from:

- Time decay
- Probability
- Repeatability
- Discipline

Not prediction.

Nugget: Systems Outperform Genius

The most successful traders don't predict—they execute.

A repeatable system beats intuition, luck, and market "feel" across years of trading.

Consistency is the real superpower.

In This Chapter, You Learned:

- The Wheel reduces risk through structure
- Assignment is part of the plan, not a failure
- Emotional mistakes are the biggest danger

- Risk is chosen before a trade

- Small premiums often mean safer trades

- The real reward comes from consistency

Part II

CORE STRATEGIES

CHAPTER 5

SELLING CASH-SECURED PUTS

Selling cash-secured puts is the foundation of the Wheel Strategy.

It's simple, powerful, and one of the safest ways to generate income in the stock market, even before you own any shares.

In this chapter, you'll learn exactly how the strategy works, why it is so effective, and how to apply it the right way.

1. What Is a Cash-Secured Put?

A cash-secured put means:

- You sell a put option
- You fully back it with cash
- You get paid upfront (premium)
- You agree to buy 100 shares if assigned

That's it.

This is *not* gambling.

This is simply saying, "I am willing to buy this stock at a lower price, and you must pay me for that agreement."

Nugget: A Limit Order That Pays You

A cash-secured put is just a limit order with a paycheck attached.

If you already want the stock at a lower price, selling a put lets you name your price—*and get paid while you wait.*

2. Why This Strategy Is So Safe

It's safe because:

- You choose the stock
- You choose the price
- You choose the probability
- You choose the expiration
- You have cash to buy shares if assigned

There is no leverage.

No margin.

No guessing.

You only sell puts on stocks you want to own anyway.

If you get assigned, you don't lose—you buy shares at a discount.

Nugget: No Assignment Surprise

Unlike buyers, put sellers always know:

- what stock they might get
- at what price
- and with how much cash required

There is no uncertainty—only choice.

3. How You Get Paid

When you sell a put, someone pays you a premium.

For example:

- Stock: $22
- Sell the $20 put for $1.00

You receive $1.00 × 100 = $100 instantly.

That $100 is yours no matter what happens.

Even if:

- the stock goes up
- the stock goes sideways
- the stock drops slightly

You keep the premium.

Only if the stock drops below $20 at expiration will you be assigned shares, and even then, you effectively bought at a discount.

Your effective cost basis = Strike – Premium.

$20 – $1 = $19

Nugget: Premium = Automatic Discount

Every put premium collected lowers your effective purchase price.

Put sellers automatically buy cheaper than market price—something share buyers *never* get.

4. Why Assignment Is Not a Bad Thing

In the Wheel Strategy, assignment is the goal.

If you're assigned:

- You now own 100 shares
- At a price you pre-selected
- At a discount thanks to the premium

Then the next step is simple. Sell a covered call on those shares → collect more income.

You're now in the second half of the Wheel.

5. How to Choose the Right Strike Price

Professional sellers use delta to select strikes.

Common choices:

- Delta 0.20 → ~80% probability of profit
- Delta 0.25 → more premium, more risk
- Delta 0.30 → highest premium, highest risk

Safer strikes = OTM (below stock price).

Greedy strikes = ATM or ITM (don't do this starting out).

Nugget: Delta = Risk Dial

Delta isn't magic—it's just a risk knob you turn up or down.

Lower delta = safer trade.

Higher delta = more premium but more assignment risk.

You choose the balance.

6. How to Choose the Right Expiration

Most income traders use:

- 7–10 days (weeklies) for fast theta decay
- 14–16 days for safer trades with decent premium
- 30–45 days for the best balance of time decay and pricing models

Shorter time = faster profits.

Longer time = more stable pricing.

7. What Happens If the Trade Goes Against You?

If the stock drops:

- The put increases in value

- Your probability of assignment increases

You still have three choices:

1. Let assignment happen

2. Roll the put down and out (collect more credit)

3. Close the trade early

Rolling is the most common, and you'll learn that in detail later.

Nugget: You Only Lose If You Panic

A put that moves against you isn't a loss—it's a decision point.

Assignment, rolling, or closing are all valid outcomes.

The only true mistake is freaking out and breaking the plan.

8. A Real Example

Let's say:

- Stock: $18.50

- Sell the $17.50 put

- Premium collected: $0.75

You receive $75 instantly.

Possible Outcomes:

Outcome 1: Stock stays above $17.50

You keep:

- The premium

- Your cash

- And you repeat next week

Outcome 2: Stock drops below $17.50

- You are assigned 100 shares at $17.50
- Your real cost is $17.50 – $0.75 = $16.75.

You basically bought the stock at a discount, and now you sell covered calls.

In This Chapter, You Learned:

- Cash-secured puts generate income before owning shares
- You choose every part of the trade
- Assignment is good: it starts the Wheel
- Premium lowers your cost basis
- Delta determines probability
- Shorter expirations = faster income
- You can roll puts to reduce risk or extend the trade

CHAPTER 6

COVERED CALLS AND THE WHEEL

Covered calls are the second half of the Wheel Strategy, and the part where you start generating steady, repeatable income from shares you already own.

In this chapter, you will learn exactly how covered calls work, how they fit into the Wheel Strategy, and how to use them to lower your cost basis while generating consistent profit.

1. What Is a Covered Call?

A covered call means:

- You own 100 shares of a stock
- You sell a call option on those shares
- You get paid a premium
- You agree to sell your shares at the strike price if assigned

That's it.

You are covered because you already own the shares. There is no risk of losing more shares than you own.

Nugget: Rental Income on Your Shares

Think of a covered call as renting out your shares.

You own the asset.

Someone pays you for the right to use it for a short time.

If they don't use it, you collect rent again next week.

2. Why Covered Calls Are So Effective

When you sell a call option:

- You earn income instantly
- You lower your cost basis
- You reduce your downside risk
- You profit even if the stock goes nowhere

Covered calls are ideal for:

- Sideways markets
- Slightly bearish markets
- Choppy markets

You continue generating income regardless of the stock direction.

Nugget: Cost Basis Drops Every Time

Every covered call premium reduces your effective share cost.

Over time, this can turn a losing stock into a winning position simply through premium collected.

3. How Covered Calls Fit Into the Wheel

The Wheel Strategy works like this:

1. Sell a cash-secured put
2. If assigned, you own 100 shares
3. Sell a covered call on those shares
4. If your shares get called away, start over and sell another put

It's a never-ending loop of income:

Puts → Shares → Covered Calls → Back to Puts → Repeat

This is why it's called the Wheel.

Nugget: The Wheel Never Stops Paying You

Whether the stock moves up, down, or sideways, one of the two halves of the Wheel is always generating income.

4. Choosing the Right Strike Price

Again, delta helps guide your decisions.

Typical deltas for covered calls:

- Delta 0.20–0.30 → higher probability the shares *won't* be called away
- Delta 0.35–0.50 → higher premium but higher chance of assignment
- Delta 0.10–0.15 → safer but lower premium

Most Wheel traders choose between 0.20 and 0.30 for consistency.

Nugget: Strike Price Controls Your Future

Your strike determines:

- how much room the stock can run
- how much premium you earn
- and how likely assignment becomes

Choosing the right strike is choosing the right outcome.

5. Choosing the Right Expiration

Covered calls work well with:

- 7–10 days (weeklies) → fast income
- 14–16 days → safer, more stable premiums
- 30 days → smoother time decay

Shorter time = faster theta

Longer time = less volatility

Nugget: Time Is Your Friend

Covered call sellers benefit every single day—weekends included—because theta decay works nonstop.

6. What Happens If the Stock Moves?

Stock Goes Up

- Your call increases in value
- You might get assigned
- Assignment = you sell your shares at the strike price
- You still keep the premium

This is profitable, not a loss.

Stock Goes Sideways

Best outcome for covered calls.

The call:

- Loses value due to theta
- Expires worthless
- You keep the premium
- You sell another call

Repeat for more income.

Stock Goes Down

- Call becomes worthless faster
- You still keep the premium

If the stock drops too far, you can:

- Roll the call down
- Roll out in time
- Combine both
- Stop selling calls until the price recovers

But the premium you collected still lowered your cost basis.

Nugget: You Win in Three Directions

Covered calls profit when the stock:

- goes up (you sell shares at a gain)
- goes sideways (you keep shares and premium)
- goes down slightly (premium cushions the drop)

Few strategies offer this many winning scenarios.

7. Example Covered Call

Let's say:

- You own 100 shares at $19
- You sell the $20 call
- You receive $0.60 premium

That's $60 income instantly.

Outcome 1: Stock Stays Below $20

- You keep the premium
- You keep the shares
- You sell another call

Outcome 2: Stock Rises Above $20

- Shares get called away at $20
- Your profit = ($20 − $19) + $0.60
- Total = $1.60 per share = **$160**
- You start the Wheel again by selling a put

Either way, you win.

8. The #1 Rule for Covered Calls

Never sell a covered call on a stock you are not willing to sell.

If you must keep the shares (long-term investment, tax reasons, etc.) use a higher strike or lower delta to avoid assignment.

Nugget: Assignment Isn't Losing—It's Getting Paid Twice

If your shares get called away, you make money from:

1. The premium
2. The stock appreciation up to the strike

That's a double profit—not a mistake.

In This Chapter, You Learned:

- Covered calls generate income on shares you already own
- They are the second half of the Wheel
- Strike and delta selection determine assignment probability
- Theta decay benefits you every day
- You profit whether the stock moves up, sideways, or down slightly
- Assignment is not a loss, it's part of the Wheel

CHAPTER 7

MANAGING POSITIONS

Selling options for income isn't just about entering trades, it's about managing them with confidence and discipline.

Most problems arise not from bad trades, but from poor management once the trade is on.

In this chapter, you'll learn exactly how to manage your puts and calls like a professional.

1. Always Know Your Exit Before You Enter

Before selling any option, ask yourself:

- What will I do if the stock goes up?
- What will I do if the stock goes sideways?
- What will I do if the stock goes down?
- Will I roll? Close early? Accept assignment?

If you know your plan ahead of time, you eliminate emotional decision-making.

Nugget: A Plan Beats Prediction

Professional traders don't predict outcomes—they prepare for them.

When you know all three possible paths before entering, no movement in the market can surprise you.

2. The 50% Rule: Take Profits Early

One of the smartest habits in options selling is to take profits when the option reaches 50% of maximum gain.

Example:

- You sell a put for $1.00
- When it drops to $0.50
- Buy it back
- Lock in profits
- Sell a new put immediately

This creates faster turnover, more consistency, and lower risk.

Nugget: 50% Win Rate Boost

Studies on tens of thousands of trades show that closing at 50%:

- Increases win rate
- Reduces drawdowns
- Decreases time in each trade
- Improves monthly income stability

The 50% rule is one of the most powerful habits in premium selling.

3. When to Close a Trade Early

Close a position early if:

- The premium has decayed significantly (50–70%)
- The trade is taking too long to move
- IV is dropping quickly
- The stock is drifting away from the strike
- Earnings are approaching and you want to avoid volatility

Closing early keeps your capital working.

Nugget: Time Is Money—Don't Waste It

If your capital is tied up in a slow trade, it can't earn income elsewhere.

Premium sellers win by turning over trades, not by waiting forever for the last few dollars of premium.

4. When to Roll a Losing Position

Rolling means:

- Closing the current trade
- Opening a new one
- For more time, lower strike, and/or more credit

Rolling is ideal when:

- The stock has moved against you
- You want to avoid assignment
- You want to lower your break-even
- You want to stay in the trade longer

You'll learn advanced rolling techniques in later chapters.

Nugget: Rolling Buys Time and Lowers Risk

A roll can:

- Push out expiration
- Move the strike farther from danger
- Reduce your cost basis
- Convert a losing trade into a winning one

Rolling is your ultimate risk-management tool.

5. When to Let Assignment Happen

Assignment is *not* a failure.

It is a normal part of the Wheel Strategy.

Accept assignment when:

- You chose the stock willingly
- You want to transition to covered calls
- You don't mind owning at the strike
- Rolling no longer improves your cost basis

Assignment gives you the shares you were planning to own anyway, often at a discount due to the premium received.

Nugget: Assignment = Opportunity

Assignment doesn't stop your income—it changes where your income comes from.

Once assigned, you simply switch to covered calls and continue collecting premium.

6. When to Not Sell Anything

Sometimes, the best move is wait.

Examples:

- Stock is extremely volatile
- Chart is unclear
- Premiums are unusually low
- Your position size is too big
- Your account needs to cool down

Patience is a position.

Discipline is a position.

Cash is a position.

Waiting protects your capital.

Nugget: Cash Is a Position—and a Powerful One

Cash is not "doing nothing."

Cash gives you:

- Flexibility
- Patience
- Protection
- Opportunity to strike at the right moment

Smart traders know when *not* to trade.

7. Keep Trades Small and Manageable

Never let one position dominate your account.

General guideline:

- No single Wheel position should exceed 20% of your account.
- Smaller positions = easier management.
- Big positions = stressful decisions.

You want a calm, sustainable income system, not emotional swings.

Nugget: Small Sizes Keep You in the Game

Most blown-up accounts fail not due to strategy errors, but because the trader went too big on one trade.

Small sizes = survivability.

Survivability = long-term income.

8. Review Your Trades Weekly

Professional traders review:

- Wins
- Losses
- Rolls
- Mistakes
- Opportunities

A simple weekly review dramatically improves your results.

Ask:

- Did I follow my plan?
- Was my position size appropriate?
- Did I enter for the right reasons?
- Did I roll too early or too late?
- Did emotions influence my choices?

Awareness improves results.

Nugget: Review = Growth

A weekly review turns experience into expertise.

You learn more from analyzing a losing trade than winning ten trades in a row.

In This Chapter, You Learned:

- Always plan exits before entering trades
- Take profits early at 50%
- Close trades when they've decayed enough
- Roll positions when appropriate
- Assignment is normal in the Wheel
- Sometimes it's best to wait
- Position size determines stress and success
- Regular reviews improve discipline

CHAPTER 8

ROLLING OPTIONS LIKE A PRO

Rolling is one of the most important skills in options selling.

It allows you to turn losing positions into winning ones, extend time, reduce risk, and collect additional income—all without closing the position at a loss.

When done correctly, rolling can dramatically improve your profitability and keep your Wheel Strategy running smoothly.

1. What Does It Mean to Roll an Option?

Rolling is a two-part transaction:

1. Buy to close your current option
2. Sell to open a new option

This new option can be:

- Further out in time (rolling out)
- At a different strike price (rolling down or up)
- Or both (rolling out and down/up)

The goal of rolling is simple: Improve your position.

__Nugget: Rolling = Staying in Control__

When you roll, you're not saving a trade—you're redesigning it.

Rolling lets you adjust time, strike, and risk so the market must work *for* you, not against you.

2. When Should You Roll a Put?

You roll a put when:

- The stock drops below your strike
- You want to avoid assignment
- You want more time for the stock to recover
- You want to lower your break-even price

Rolling allows you to:

- Push the assignment decision into the future
- Collect additional credit
- Move to a safer strike

__Nugget: Rolling Buys Time, Literally__

Time is the most valuable asset in option selling.

Rolling a put gives the stock room to recover while paying you more premium.

3. When Should You Roll a Call?

You roll a covered call when:

- The stock is approaching or surpassing your strike
- You want to keep your shares
- You want to collect more premium
- You want to move to a higher strike

This helps you avoid assignment while generating additional income.

Nugget: Rolling Saves Your Shares

If your goal is long-term ownership, rolling a call is the tool that lets you avoid selling too early—while still collecting premium every week.

4. The Three Types of Rolls

1. Roll Out (Same Strike, More Time)

Use this when:

- Stock is near your strike
- You want to avoid immediate assignment
- You want additional premium

You push the expiration out without changing the strike.

2. Roll Down (Lower Strike, Same Expiration)

Use this when:

- You want a safer strike
- You want to reduce risk
- You are OK with potentially increasing assignment probability

Rolling down a put lowers your break-even.

3. Roll Out and Down (More Time + Safer Strike)

This is the best defensive roll for puts.

Used when:

- Stock has moved significantly against you
- You want a lower strike
- You need more time
- You still want to collect credit

You improve both time and strike simultaneously.

Nugget: Combine Time + Strike = Maximum Safety

Rolling out and down is the equivalent of hitting the reset button, with more premium, more safety, and more time added to your side.

5. Rolling for a Net Credit: The Golden Rule

The #1 rule of rolling: Always roll for a net credit whenever possible.

If you roll for a credit:

- You collect more money
- Your break-even improves
- Your cost basis drops
- Your probability of success increases

Rolling for a debit should be rare and only used in special situations.

A debit roll increases your cost basis and reduces the power of the Wheel Strategy.

As a general rule, you should never pay to make a trade worse unless you're gaining something strategically valuable in return.

Debits are justified only when:

- You need to protect shares you do not want called away
- The debit allows you to move to a much safer strike
- The debit sets up a stronger premium opportunity next cycle
- You are avoiding a short-term event (like earnings) that would force an unfavorable assignment
- The debit is tiny compared to the overall premium collected so far

Use debit rolls sparingly.

They are tools—not habits.

Nugget: Credits Build a Safety Cushion

Every credit increases the buffer between you and a losing trade.

The more credits you stack, the harder it becomes for a trade to go against you.

6. How Rolling Reduces Break-Even

Example:

- You sell a put for $1.00
- Stock drops
- You roll out and down, collecting $0.40 credit

Your new total premium = $1.00 + $0.40 = $1.40.

If your strike is $20, your new break-even = $20 – $1.40 = $18.60.

Rolling literally moves your position in your favor by improving time, strike, and total premium collected.

Nugget: Rolling Is Cost-Basis Engineering

Every roll reshapes your cost basis.

The more premium you collect, the farther you push your break-even away from danger.

7. Rolling Covered Calls Upward

If the stock runs up:

- Rolling up and out lets you keep your shares
- You move to a higher strike
- You collect more premium
- You give the stock more room

Example:

- You sold a $25 call
- Stock runs to $27
- You roll to the $28 strike for next week
- You collect a credit
- You avoid assignment

Rolling gives you flexibility.

Nugget: Rolling Keeps You in the Trend

When a stock is running, rolling your covered call lets you stay in the trend rather than getting forced out at a lower price.

8. When Not to Roll

Do *not* roll when:

- The stock is fundamentally breaking down
- IV is collapsing
- You're forcing a losing position for no reason
- Assignment would be better
- Rolling costs too much (large debit)

Sometimes the best move is to accept assignment and move to the next step of the Wheel.

Nugget: Avoid Zombie Trades

A zombie trade is one you keep rolling even though the stock's fundamentals are collapsing.

Rolling only works if the company is strong—not dying.

9. Rolling Turns You Into a Professional

Professionals rarely let positions expire untouched.

They're constantly:

- Rolling
- Managing
- Improving strikes
- Extending time
- Collecting credit
- Reducing cost basis

Rolling is how you engineer your trades to maximize probability.

Nugget: Pros Don't Panic—They Adjust

The difference between amateurs and professionals isn't their strategy…

It's their ability to adjust positions calmly and systematically.

Rolling gives you that power.

In This Chapter, You Learned:

- What rolling is
- When to roll puts and calls
- The three types of rolls
- Why rolling for credit is essential
- How rolling lowers break-even
- How rolling helps keep shares during a rally
- When not to roll
- Rolling is a professional trader's tool

CHAPTER 9

UNDERSTANDING THETA DECAY

Theta decay, also known as time decay, is the single most important concept for an options seller.

If you understand theta, you understand why selling options works, why income is consistent, and why the Wheel Strategy is so powerful.

When buyers lose money from the passage of time, sellers gain money.

This chapter puts theta decay into simple, real-world terms.

1. What Is Theta?

Theta measures how much an option loses in value each day simply because time is passing.

Example: If an option has a theta of –0.08, that means it loses 8 cents per day, or $0.08 × 100 shares = $8 per day of natural decay.

If you sold that option, you are gaining this value as the option loses it.

Nugget: Theta Is Guaranteed Decay

Theta is one of the few *predictable* forces in the market.

Price may move up or down, volatility may rise or fall, but time will always pass, and theta will always work in your favor as a seller.

2. Why Time Works Against Buyers but For You

Option buyers need something to happen:

- The stock must move fast
- The stock must move far
- It must happen before expiration

Sellers, on the other hand, only need:

- Time to pass
- The stock to not crash
- Price to stay near or OTM

You win by waiting.

Nugget: Buyers Need to Be Right—Sellers Just Need to Be Patient

A buyer must be correct on direction + magnitude + timing.

A seller only needs the clock to keep ticking.

3. Theta Decay Accelerates as Expiration Approaches

This is the key advantage for weekly sellers.

Here's how time decay works:

- 45 days out → slow decay
- 30 days out → medium decay
- Under 14 days → fast decay
- Last 7 days → extremely fast decay

This is why many income traders use:

- 7–10 day expirations
- 14–16 day expirations

The last few days before expiration deliver the fastest decay.

Nugget: The Sweet Spot Is 7–16 Days

This window delivers the best balance of fast decay, consistent premium, and manageable risk, which is why so many income traders prefer it.

4. The Time Decay Curve (Simple Explanation)

Imagine a curve that starts out flat, then drops sharply as it approaches expiration.

That's theta. The option loses value slowly at first, then rapidly:

Slow → Medium → Fast → Very Fast → Expiration

If you are selling options, you want to be on the right side of this curve.

Nugget: The Curve Always Bends Toward Zero

Extrinsic value must reach zero at expiration.

As a seller, you are collecting that disappearing value day by day.

5. Why Selling OTM Options Maximizes Theta

OTM (Out of the Money) options:

- Are mostly extrinsic value
- Have no intrinsic value
- Decay faster
- Carry high probability of expiring worthless

This is where income sellers make their money—that slow-then-rapid evaporation of extrinsic value.

Nugget: Pure Extrinsic = Pure Income

OTM options are almost entirely extrinsic value, and extrinsic is the part that disappears, which means it's the part you profit from.

6. Why Theta Favors the Wheel Strategy

When you sell:

- Cash-secured puts
- Covered calls

You are collecting extrinsic value.

And extrinsic value disappears over time.

This means the Wheel Strategy is built on:

- High probability
- Rapid decay
- Repeated income

It is perfectly aligned with theta.

7. Example of How Theta Pays You

Let's say you sell a put for:

- Premium: $1.00
- With theta = −0.07

Every day, the option naturally loses 7 cents:

$0.07 × 100 = $7 per day

You don't have to do anything.

You simply collect the decay as income.

After a week, that's $49 of decay, even if the stock price barely moved.

Nugget: Theta Pays Even When the Stock Sleeps

Your stock doesn't need to move for you to profit. Theta decay alone can deliver the majority of your weekly income.

8. Theta Helps You Win by Losing

Even if the stock goes slightly against you, theta helps offset the movement.

Example:

- Stock dips slightly

- Put increases a little

- But theta decay offsets some of that increase

This means many trades recover on their own, simply through the passage of time.

Nugget: Time Heals Many Trades

A position that looks red today may turn green tomorrow, not from price action but from theta erosion.

9. The Only Time Theta Doesn't Help You

When you are buying options.

Buyers are constantly losing value as time passes.

This is why we sell, not buy.

In This Chapter, You Learned:

- Theta is the daily decay of option value

- Time works against buyers and for sellers

- Decay accelerates as expiration approaches

- OTM options deliver the fastest decay

- The Wheel Strategy thrives on time decay

- Theta helps you win by waiting

- Selling, not buying, benefits from theta

CHAPTER 10

COMBINING STRATEGIES

Once you understand cash-secured puts and covered calls, you have the foundation of the Wheel Strategy.

But there are times when combining strategies can help you reduce risk, increase probability, or smooth out your income flow.

This chapter shows you simple, effective combinations—nothing overly complex—that you can begin using immediately.

1. The Power of Keeping It Simple

Before we begin, remember:

- The Wheel Strategy itself is already extremely powerful.
- You do *not* need to learn 20 strategies to be successful.

The purpose of combining strategies is *not* to get fancy but to:

- Reduce risk
- Improve consistency
- Manage losing positions better
- Smooth out income

Everything here supports the Wheel. Nothing replaces it.

Nugget: Complexity Rarely Improves Results

Most traders lose money not because they lack strategies, but because they use too many.

Professional income traders master a few tools deeply—and repeat them.

2. Put + Call: The Full Wheel Cycle

The most basic combination is simply:

1. Sell a cash-secured put
2. Get assigned → own shares
3. Sell a covered call

That's two strategies working together to generate income.

Professionals repeat this cycle endlessly. It's simple. It works. It builds wealth.

Nugget: The Wheel = Controlled Recurring Income

Most strategies rely on predicting direction.

The Wheel relies on structure and repetition, which is why it outperforms prediction-based strategies over time.

3. The Put Ladder (Safer Entry Into Shares)

A put ladder means selling multiple puts at different strikes and/or expirations.

Example:

- Sell a $20 put for next Friday
- Sell a $19.50 put for two weeks out
- Sell an $18.50 put for three weeks out

Why do this?

- You collect three sets of premiums
- You spread your entry prices
- You avoid being assigned all shares at one price
- You reduce risk if the stock drifts downward

This is a professional technique for smoother entries.

Nugget: Laddering Reduces Timing Risk

Selling puts at staggered strikes avoids committing all your cash at one moment—a key technique used by professionals to average into positions safely.

4. The Call Ladder (Smoother Covered Call Income)

If you own multiple sets of shares (200, 300, 500 shares), you can sell covered calls at different strikes.

Example with 300 shares:

- 1 contract at $22
- 1 contract at $23
- 1 contract at $24

This spreads risk and creates:

- More flexibility
- Multiple income opportunities
- Lower probability of all shares being called away

This technique protects your long-term share holdings better than selling one aggressive strike.

Nugget: Ladders Give You Flex While Keeping Premium Flowing

A call ladder lets you capture premium at several price levels, so you can profit even when the stock drifts unpredictably.

5. The Put + Call Combo (For Sideways Markets)

When a stock trades in a clear channel, you can combine:

- A cash-secured put
- A covered call

Example:

- Sell a $20 put
- Sell a $24 call once assigned

This captures premium from both sides of the price range as the stock bounces.

This is simply the Wheel Strategy operating in a tight band—extremely effective for stocks with strong support and resistance levels.

Nugget: Sideways Markets Are an Income Seller's Playground

While directional traders struggle, Wheel traders capitalize—every bounce generates new premium on one side or the other.

6. The Premium Boost Roll Strategy

This happens when the stock goes against you.

Example:

- You sell the $20 put
- Stock drops to $19
- Instead of accepting assignment immediately…
- You roll out and down to a lower strike and collect more credit

This combines:

- Rolling
- Strike improvement
- Time decay
- Additional premium

It is a powerful way to avoid taking shares too early while lowering your break-even.

Nugget: Boosting Premium = Buying More Safety

Adding credits through rolls lowers your cost basis and increases your probability of profit. Stacked credits create a cushion against volatility.

7. The Extended Wheel (For Investors Who Love the Stock)

If you truly want to accumulate shares:

1. Sell a put
2. Get assigned
3. Sell a covered call
4. Get called away
5. Sell another put
6. Target assignment again
7. Sell covered calls again

Instead of one Wheel cycle, you intentionally run multiple Wheels on the same stock.

This works extremely well on:

- High-IV stocks
- Reliable growth stocks
- Stocks you'd hold long-term anyway

Nugget: Extended Wheel = Compounding Premium + Ownership

Running multiple Wheel cycles on a quality stock can dramatically lower your long-term cost basis while still producing weekly or monthly income.

8. Combining Strategies Reduces Emotional Pressure

Here's an overlooked point. When you combine strategies:

- You have more choices
- You panic less
- You never feel trapped
- You always have a rational next step
- You remain calm and logical

This is the mindset of a professional options seller.

Nugget: More Tools = Less Emotion

The more strategic options you have, the less likely you are to make impulsive decisions.

Confidence comes from choices, not predictions.

In This Chapter, You Learned:

- Combining strategies doesn't mean complexity
- Put + Call = Wheel
- Ladders smooth out risk
- Put + Call combos work well in sideways markets
- Rolling improves positions
- The Extended Wheel builds long-term wealth
- More tools = more confidence and less emotion

Part III

ADVANCED TECHNIQUES

CHAPTER 11

ROLLING FOR CREDIT AND PROBABILITY

Rolling for credit and rolling for probability are two of the most powerful techniques used by professional options traders.

These methods allow you to:

- Stay in control of risk

- Improve your break-even

- Keep trades alive longer

- Turn potential losers into long-term winners

This chapter breaks down how to apply these advanced rolling concepts the same way pros do, in simple language.

1. The Goal of Rolling Isn't to Avoid Losing: It's to Improve Probability

When beginners roll a trade, they often think, *I'm rolling to avoid losing.*

Professionals think, *I'm rolling to improve the probability of winning.*

This is a massive mental shift. Rolling isn't fear, it's strategy.

Nugget: Rolling Is Offensive, Not Defensive

Amateurs roll because they feel trapped.

Professionals roll because they're improving their odds, not escaping danger.

2. The Three Improvements Every Roll Should Create

A good roll should achieve at least one of the following:

1. Collect more credit

2. Move to a safer strike

3. Add more time for the trade to recover

A great roll achieves all three at once.

Example:

- Original trade: Sell $20 put for $1.00

- Roll out and down to $19 strike for next week

- Collect an additional $0.40

New total premium: $1.40

New break-even: $17.60

This is rolling like a pro.

Nugget: Each Roll Should Make the Trade Better Than Before

If the roll doesn't improve strike, premium, or time, it's not a professional roll.

3. Rolling for Credit (The Golden Method)

Rolling for credit means:

- Your closing order costs something

- But your new opening order pays more

- And you net positive

This is ideal.

Why credits are powerful:

- Your break-even improves
- Your cost basis drops
- Your probability of success increases
- You are paid for extending the trade

Always try to roll for a net credit when possible.

Nugget: Credits Build a Cushion

Each additional credit creates a thicker padding between you and a losing trade.

Eventually, your total premium collected can outweigh even major price drops.

4. Rolling for Probability (The Safety Method)

Sometimes you take a small debit, but gain a much safer strike.

Example:

- Stock drops heavily
- You sell the $20 put
- Price falls to $17
- You roll out and down to an $18 strike
- You take a small debit to get there

Your probability of success dramatically improves.

This is rolling for safety, not profit.

Both credit and probability rolls have value.

Nugget: A Safer Strike Is Sometimes Worth Paying For

If a small debit increases your probability dramatically, you're buying better odds—not losing money.

5. When to Roll Early vs. Late

Roll early when:

- The stock is slowly drifting against you
- Premiums are still high
- IV is elevated
- You want more time fast

Roll late when:

- The stock has already dropped sharply
- There is little extrinsic value left
- You want to avoid assignment at the last minute

Both timing methods have their place, but rolling early usually produces better results.

Nugget: Early Rolls Give You More Choices

The earlier you adjust, the more premium remains and the easier it is to engineer a winning roll.

6. How to Roll a Put Like a Professional

Here's the process pros follow:

1. Close the current put
2. Pick a lower strike
3. Push expiration out 7–30 days
4. Make sure you're rolling for a credit, if possible
5. Enter the new trade

Your new position is safer, stronger, and more profitable.

Nugget: Professional Rolls Always Improve the Position

If the new strike, premium, or timeframe isn't better, professionals simply don't roll yet.

7. How to Roll a Call Like a Professional

Covered call rolling has a different goal:

- Keep your shares
- Move to a higher strike
- Collect more credit
- Extend the trade

Example:

- Sold $25 call
- Stock runs to $26.50
- You roll to $26 or $27 strike for next week
- Collect credit
- Keep the shares

This is how you continue running the Wheel and avoid losing shares too early.

Nugget: Rolling Calls = Protecting Your Shares While Getting Paid

With calls, rolling isn't about survival—it's about strategically delaying assignment while stacking more premium.

8. What to Avoid When Rolling

Do *not* roll:

- If rolling costs a massive debit
- On weak, falling stocks
- Into earnings week (volatility spike risk)
- To a strike too close to the money
- Without checking IV and delta

Rolling should improve your position, not trap you in a bad one.

Nugget: Not Every Trade Should Be Saved

Sometimes the best decision is to accept assignment, reposition, or move on.

Professionals avoid zombie trades—positions kept alive when they shouldn't be.

9. Rolling Helps You Win the Long Game

Professional sellers don't fight the market.

They work with the market.

Rolling allows you to:

- Be patient
- Improve probability
- Build better positions
- Avoid panic
- Turn short-term pressure into long-term income

Rolling isn't a trick.

It's a mindset.

Nugget: Rolling Turns Volatility into Opportunity

Most traders fear volatility.

Premium sellers use it to create better strikes, bigger credits, and safer positions through strategic rolls.

In This Chapter, You Learned:

- Rolling improves credit, probability, or time
- Rolling for credit is ideal
- Rolling for probability is safer
- Early rolls often work best
- Rolling puts and calls follow different rules
- Avoid rolling into bad conditions
- Rolling helps you win consistently

CHAPTER 12

SPREADS, LADDERS, AND MULTI-LEG TRADES

You already know the Wheel Strategy can create consistent income using the simplest possible trades: selling puts and selling calls.

But sometimes, you'll want more control, less risk, or a more flexible way to manage a trade—and that's where spreads, ladders, and multi-leg setups become useful.

This chapter explains these advanced strategies in a simple, no-math, no-jargon style so you can add them to your toolbox confidently.

1. Why Use Multi-Leg Trades?

Multi-leg setups allow you to:

- Reduce risk
- Control assignment
- Manage large price moves
- Create defined-risk positions
- Smooth income across multiple strikes
- Build advanced versions of the Wheel

They're optional, not required, but incredibly helpful once you're comfortable selling options.

Nugget: Multi-Leg Trades Increase Control—Not Complexity

The purpose of a multi-leg strategy isn't to look sophisticated.

It's to give you more ways to shape risk and reward so you never feel trapped in a trade.

GOOD EXAMPLE—Multi-Leg for Control

A stock is stable but single-leg premiums are tiny.

You use a credit spread to define risk and boost probability.

Result: Steady, safe income.

BAD EXAMPLE—Multi-Leg in High Volatility

Trader opens an iron condor right before earnings.

Stock gaps massively → one side hits max loss.

2. The Vertical Spread (Defined-Risk Income)

A vertical spread is a combination of two options:

- You sell one option
- You buy another option
- Both share the same expiration
- But they use different strikes

There are two basic types for sellers:

1. Put Credit Spread

- Sell higher strike put
- Buy lower strike put
- Collect a net credit
- Max loss is defined

This is a safer version of selling cash-secured puts.

2. Call Credit Spread

- Sell lower strike call
- Buy higher strike call
- Collect a net credit
- Defined risk

This is a safer version of selling covered calls when you don't own shares.

Nugget: Spreads Cap Your Risk Automatically

Vertical spreads transform unlimited or large risk trades into defined-risk trades, making them ideal for small accounts and volatile markets.

GOOD EXAMPLE—Put Credit Spread

Stock at $50

Sell $48 put / buy $45 put

Stock stays above $48 → full credit earned.

BAD EXAMPLE—Put Credit Spread

Unexpected news drops stock to $42 → spread hits max loss.

3. When to Use Vertical Spreads

Use vertical spreads when:

- You want defined risk
- Premiums are small
- Stock is too expensive to sell naked puts
- You want a safer alternative to the Wheel

Vertical spreads are popular for traders with smaller accounts or during volatile markets.

Nugget: Spreads Let You Trade Expensive Stocks Cheaply

With a credit spread, you can trade stocks like NVDA or TSLA.

without needing thousands in buying power.

GOOD EXAMPLE—Expensive Stock Workaround

TSLA at $300 → CSP too expensive → use a $300/$290 put spread.

BAD EXAMPLE—Low Volatility Problems

Low IV = tiny credits → spreads become poor risk/reward.

4. The Ladder Strategy (Steady, Diversified Income)

A ladder means placing multiple trades at different:

- Strikes
- Expirations
- Delta levels

This creates:

- More frequent income
- Less volatility
- More defensive positioning

Example put ladder:

- $20 put (1 week)
- $19.50 put (2 weeks)
- $19 put (3 weeks)

Nugget: Ladders Reduce Timing Risk

Instead of trying to guess the best moment, ladders let you enter gradually, smoothing your entry and reducing emotional pressure.

GOOD EXAMPLE—Smooth Entry

Stock drifts downward → each ladder strike offers a better price.

BAD EXAMPLE—Rapid Selloff

Stock collapses from $20 → $12 → all puts become problematic at once.

5. The Layered Wheel (Advanced Version of the Wheel)

Instead of running one Wheel cycle, the Layered Wheel runs multiple Wheels across:

- Different stocks
- Different deltas
- Different expirations

This creates:

- Weekly income
- Monthly income
- High probability exposure
- Defensive flexibility

You're essentially running a portfolio of Wheels.

Nugget: Multiple Wheels = Multiple Income Streams

Just like diversifying rental properties, multiple Wheels create multiple rent checks through option premium.

GOOD EXAMPLE—Diversified Wheels

Running Wheels on KO, PLTR, and AMD spreads risk and smooths income.

BAD EXAMPLE—All Wheels on One Ticker

Running 3 Wheels on RIVN → stock craters → oversized assignment.

6. The Strangle (Premium from Both Sides)

A short strangle means:

- Sell OTM put
- Sell OTM call
- Same expiration
- Collect premium on both sides

Use only on:

- High-IV stocks
- Stable ranges
- With experience

Risk is unlimited on the upside.

Nugget: Strangles Offer High Income but High Responsibility

A strangle pays extremely well because you take on more risk.

It should only be used by traders with discipline and proper margin.

GOOD EXAMPLE—Range-Bound Stock

Stock stays between your put and call → double premium earned.

BAD EXAMPLE—Explosive Move

Stock jumps from \$50 → \$70 → call side explodes in loss.

7. The Iron Condor (Defined-Risk Strangle)

The iron condor is the safer version of the strangle:

- Sell OTM put
- Sell OTM call
- Buy a lower put
- Buy a higher call

Collect two premiums and define risk on both sides.

Nugget: Iron Condors Thrive in Boring Markets

If the stock trades in a tight range, condors generate income with very little management.

GOOD EXAMPLE—Sideways Action

Stock drifts mildly → both spreads expire worthless → full credit.

BAD EXAMPLE—Earnings Shock

Stock gaps beyond your call wing → call spread hits max loss.

8. Why Multi-Leg Trades Matter Even If You Never Use Them

Even if you never trade spreads or condors, understanding them helps you:

- Think more strategically
- Manage Wheel positions better
- Understand hedging
- Improve your rolling decisions

These tools expand your competence as a trader even before you place your first advanced trade.

Nugget: Knowledge = Confidence

Knowing *how* these tools work means you always have options even if you never use them.

GOOD EXAMPLE—Better Decisions

Understanding condors helps you avoid selling naked calls during low volatility.

BAD EXAMPLE—Trading Without Understanding

A new trader enters a strangle without knowing assignment mechanics → disaster.

In This Chapter, You Learned:

- Why multi-leg trades exist
- How credit spreads define risk
- How ladders create smoother income
- How the Layered Wheel works
- What strangles and condors do
- How advanced tools improve your trading philosophy

CHAPTER 13

THE PSYCHOLOGY OF THE PROFESSIONAL SELLER

Develop the mindset that separates consistent traders from gamblers. Selling options successfully is not about intelligence, secret indicators, or predicting the market.

It's about behavior.

Two traders can use the same strategy, the same stock, and the same strikes—one builds steady income, the other blows up.

The difference is mindset.

This chapter shows you how professional option sellers think, act, and respond to the market so you can trade with clarity, discipline, and long-term confidence.

1. Professionals Think in Probabilities, Not Predictions

Gamblers ask:

- "Is this stock going to explode?"
- "What if this moons?"
- "What if this crashes?"

Professional sellers ask:

- "What is the probability this trade succeeds?"
- "Is the premium worth the risk?"
- "Does this fit my system?"

You are not trying to be right.

You are trying to be paid for probability.

Nugget: You Don't Need to Be Right to Make Money

Option sellers can be wrong on direction and still win.

Time decay, distance from the strike, and premium do the work, not prediction.

2. Consistency Beats Excitement

The market rewards boring behavior.

Professional sellers:

- Sell similar deltas
- Trade similar expirations
- Use the same checklist
- Repeat the same process

Gamblers:

- Chase premium
- Change rules weekly
- Oversize trades
- Trade for adrenaline

Excitement feels good.

Consistency builds accounts.

Nugget: If a Trade Feels Exciting, It's Probably Risky

Calm trades compound.

Emotional trades destroy discipline.

3. Losses Are Data, Not Failure

Losses will happen:

- Puts get tested
- Calls get challenged
- Rolls become necessary
- Assignments occur

Professionals don't panic, they analyze:

- Was the strike too aggressive?
- Was IV misleading?
- Was position size too large?
- Did earnings sneak up?

Every trade is feedback.

4. Position Size Controls Emotion

Most emotional mistakes come from trading too big.

When position size is appropriate:

- Red days feel manageable
- Rolling feels logical
- Decisions remain calm
- Discipline stays intact

If you feel anxious, distracted, or stressed, the position is too large.

Nugget: Calm Is a Signal You Sized Correctly

If one trade can ruin your mood, it can ruin your account.

5. Patience Is a Profit Skill

Option selling rewards:

- Waiting for good strikes
- Letting theta work
- Giving rolls time
- Allowing assignment when appropriate

Impatience causes:

- Early closes
- Bad rolls
- Chasing premium
- Breaking rules

Time is your edge.

Use it.

6. Rules Protect You From Yourself

Your rules exist for one reason:

to save you when emotions try to take over.

Rules like:

- Delta limits
- Position sizing caps
- No earnings trades
- Defined rolling criteria
- Weekly income targets

Professionals follow rules even when they *want* to break them.

7. Detachment Creates Clarity

You are not your trade.

You are not your P/L.

You are not your last result.

Professionals:

- Focus on process, not outcome
- Judge success over months, not days
- Detach identity from trades

The market doesn't care about your feelings, but your system does.

8. Think Like a Business Owner

Businesses:

- Track performance
- Manage risk
- Accept expenses
- Improve systems
- Focus on sustainability

Your option trading is a business.

Premium is revenue.

Losses are costs.

Discipline is profit.

9. Long-Term Thinking Wins

One trade doesn't matter.

One week doesn't matter.

One bad roll doesn't matter.

What matters:

- Hundreds of trades
- Consistent rules
- Compounding premiums
- Emotional control over time

Professionals zoom out.

Gamblers zoom in.

In This Chapter, You Learned:

- Why probability matters more than prediction
- How consistency beats excitement
- Why losses are feedback, not failure
- How position size controls emotion
- Why patience is a profit skill
- How rules protect discipline
- Why detachment improves decision-making
- How to think like a trading business owner

Part IV

REAL-WORLD APPLICATION

CHAPTER 14

BUILDING YOUR OPTIONS INCOME PORTFOLIO

Now that you understand the mechanics, strategies, and psychology behind selling options, it's time to apply them in the real world.

This chapter shows you how to build a practical, stable, and scalable options income portfolio, one that supports the Wheel Strategy and pays you consistently.

1. Start With the Right Types of Stocks

The Wheel Strategy works best on:

A. Strong Companies With Real Financials

Examples:

- AMD
- HIMS
- INTC
- MU
- KO
- WMT

These stocks:

- Are liquid
- Have options with good volume
- Are less likely to collapse
- Recover from downturns

Nugget: Strong Stocks Pay You Twice

Solid companies provide:

1. Reliable premiums, and
2. Share price recovery, which makes assignments far less stressful.

The Wheel thrives on stocks that don't implode.

B. Growth Stocks With High IV

Examples:

- RGTI
- PLTR
- RIVN
- MARA (careful with crypto volatility)

These stocks:

- Pay large premiums
- Move fast
- Require careful strike selection

Use these for higher income, not long-term holdings.

Nugget: High IV = High Income and High Risk

High-IV stocks can generate *amazing* premiums, but if you're not conservative with delta, they can blow up your account just as fast.

C. Stocks You Are Willing to Own

The #1 filter of all:

If you wouldn't buy 100 shares today, don't sell a put on it.

Nugget: This Rule Saves Accounts

Every major blowup that happens to new traders comes from violating this rule.

If you don't want to own it, don't Wheel it.

2. Position Sizing: The Real Secret to Safety

This single rule will save you more money than anything else:

Never allocate more than 20% of your account to one Wheel position.

Why?

- Stocks can drop unexpectedly
- Rolling can require additional margin
- Diversification keeps emotions calm
- Multiple Wheels = smoother income

If you have $100,000:

- Max per position = $20,000
- Ideal = $10,000–$15,000

A calm trader is a profitable trader.

Nugget: Position Size Determines Survival

Most catastrophic losses in options accounts come from oversized positions, not bad trades.

Trade small enough that even a disaster feels manageable.

3. How Many Wheel Positions Should You Run?

Depending on account size:

Small Accounts ($5k–$20k)

- 1 Wheel position
- Or 1 position + 1 vertical spread

Medium Accounts ($20k–$100k)

- 2–4 Wheel positions
- Mix of safe stocks + high-IV trades

Large Accounts ($100k+)

- 4–8 Wheel positions
- Weekly income becomes very stable
- More diversification = lower stress

You're not building a portfolio…

You're building an income engine.

Nugget: More Positions = Less Emotion

One bad trade feels like a disaster when you only have one.

With multiple Wheels, individual trades barely matter.

4. Choose Your Weekly or Monthly Income Target

You must treat trading like a business.

Ask:

- How much weekly income do I want?
- How much capital do I need per position?
- What delta fits my tolerance?
- Do I want consistency or high premium?

Example:

- Income target: $500/week
- You run 4 positions
- Each needs to produce ~$125/week

That could be:

- 4 × $125/week
- Or 2 × $250/week

A professional seller knows their numbers.

Nugget: Income Targets Prevent Overtrading

Most traders get in trouble when they try to make losses back fast.

Targets keep you disciplined, controlled, and profitable.

5. Balance Your Portfolio by Volatility

This is the key to smooth results:

- Choose 2 stable stocks (low IV)
- Choose 1 moderate-IV stock
- Choose 1 high-IV stock

Why?

- Stability gives consistency
- Moderate IV gives opportunity
- High IV gives large premium

This creates a blended income stream.

Nugget: Volatility Balance = Emotional Balance

Too many high-IV positions create anxiety.

Too many safe positions minimize income.

A blend hits the sweet spot.

6. Avoid Earnings Weeks

Earnings create:

- Fast IV spikes
- Big premiums
- Massive risk

Professional sellers simply avoid them.

If earnings are approaching:

- Close the position
- Or roll beyond earnings
- Or skip that week

There will always be another trade. Don't gamble on earnings.

Nugget: Earnings Are a Trap for New Traders

Those giant premiums look irresistible…

but they're bait.

Most earnings moves are unpredictable and violent.

7. Build Your Watchlist

A professional watchlist includes:

1. Ticker
2. Price
3. IV Rank
4. Delta 20 or 30 put premiums
5. Upcoming earnings
6. Support and resistance levels

This lets you choose the best Wheel candidates quickly and confidently.

Nugget: Your Watchlist Should Save You Time

A strong watchlist cuts decision-making from 20 minutes to 20 seconds.

8. Track Your Results

Your trading log should include:

- Stock traded
- Strike price
- Premium
- Expiration
- Delta
- Reason for entry
- Outcome
- Notes for improvement

Review this weekly.

Your notes are how you turn experience into mastery.

Nugget: Traders Who Track Results Always Outperform

Journaling forces discipline and exposes patterns you can't see in the moment.

9. Your Portfolio Will Become Predictable Over Time

As you gain experience:

- You'll know which stocks behave well
- You'll know ideal strikes
- You'll know IV patterns
- You'll know weekly ranges
- You'll know how much income you can expect

This removes fear, stress, and uncertainty.

Nugget: Predictability = True Freedom

When you can reliably forecast your weekly income, you're no longer speculating. You're running a business.

The Wheel Stock Selection Checklist

Use this checklist before selling any option.

Nugget: Good Stocks Make Easy Wheels—Bad Stocks Make Nightmares

Your stock selection determines 80% of your success.

Fundamentals (Pass at Least 3/4)

- Revenue growth
- Positive trend
- Strong business model
- Not a hype-driven meme stock

Nugget: The Wheel Fails on Weak Businesses

Strong companies recover. Weak companies collapse.

Options Liquidity (Pass All)

- Tight bid/ask spreads
- Strong volume
- Weekly expirations

Nugget: Liquidity Is Silent Protection

Wide bid/ask spreads eat your profits on entry *and* exit.

Volatility Profile

- IV Rank fits your risk level
- IV is not at a dangerous extreme

Nugget: IV Is Your Premium Gauge

Higher IV = bigger paychecks, but bigger storms.

Price Behavior

- Clear ranges
- Support levels visible
- Not at euphoric highs

Nugget: Price Ranges Build Great Wheels

Sideways stocks produce the easiest premium cycles.

Wheel Suitability

- Comfortable owning 100 shares
- Premium meets your income goal
- Delta between 0.15–0.30
- Earnings more than 10 days away

Nugget: Comfort = Confidence

If you are uncomfortable owning shares, the stock is wrong.

Risk Management

- Position fits account size
- Rolling plan prepared
- Stress level: calm

Nugget: Your Stress Level Is a Signal

If you're sweating, the trade is too big.

In This Chapter, You Learned:

- How to choose the right stocks
- How to size your positions safely
- How many Wheel cycles to run
- How to set weekly income targets
- How to balance volatility for stability
- Why avoiding earnings protects your capital
- How to build and maintain a professional watchlist
- How tracking results creates real consistency
- The Wheel stock selection checklist

CHAPTER 15

SETTING WEEKLY INCOME TARGETS

Most traders sell options without a plan, hoping each trade will bring in some income.

Professionals do the opposite:

They set clear income targets, then build their trades around hitting those targets consistently.

This chapter shows you exactly how to design your weekly or monthly income plan so your trading becomes predictable and organized.

1. Trading Without a Target Is Just Guessing

If you don't know what income you're aiming for, you will:

- Sell random strikes
- Oversize risky trades
- Take unnecessary rolls
- Chase high premiums
- Let emotions guide decisions

Setting weekly income goals gives you structure, and structure brings consistency.

Nugget: Targets Turn You From a Gambler Into a Business Owner

A trader without a target reacts to the market.

A trader *with* a target builds the market around their plan.

2. Start With a Realistic Weekly Number

Your weekly target depends on:

- Account size
- Risk tolerance
- Volatility of chosen stocks
- Number of Wheel positions

Typical Targets:

$10,000 Account

- $50–$100/week

$30,000–$50,000 Account

- $150–$300/week

$100,000–$150,000 Account

- $500–$800/week

$200,000–$300,000 Account

- $1,000–$2,000/week

These are conservative, realistic income expectations.

Nugget: You Don't Need Huge Income to Win

Even modest weekly income compounds dramatically over time.

Consistency > Size.

3. How Many Positions You Need to Hit Your Goal

Example:

Goal: $400/week

Positions: 3

Target per position: ~$130

This might look like:

- $130 from a put on HIMS
- $120 from a call on AMD
- $150 from a put on RGTI

Three modest premiums = one goal hit.

Nugget: Small, Repeated Wins Add Up Fast

Trying to hit a home run every week leads to disaster.

Three singles beat one home run attempt—every time.

4. Sell Strikes That Match Your Target

Once you know how much income each position must generate, it becomes easy to choose trades.

If your target per trade is:

- $100/week → look for premiums around $1.00
- $50/week → premiums of $0.50
- $150/week → premiums of $1.50

This ensures consistency without forcing risky strikes.

Nugget: Targets Prevent Greed

When you know you only need $100…

you stop chasing the $300 risky strike.

5. Higher Income ≠ Higher Risk

A beginner mistake:

Chasing big premiums because the income looks exciting.

But high premiums often mean:

- High IV
- High volatility
- High assignment risk
- High emotional stress

Professionals choose consistent premiums, not dramatic ones.

Nugget: High Premiums Are Not Rewards, They Are Warnings

If a put is paying *too much*, it's because the market expects *danger*.

Trust the market.

6. Think in Weekly and Monthly Cycles

Your income can be structured around:

Weekly Cycles

- 7–10 day expirations
- Great for fast theta decay
- Most flexible

Semi-Weekly Cycles

- 14–16 days
- Safer
- Smoother pricing

Monthly Cycles

- 30–45 days
- Best for spreads
- Most predictable

Mixing Cycles Creates:

- Weekly income
- Monthly reliability
- Balance and flexibility

Nugget: Mix Cycles to Reduce Stress

When you stagger expirations, you never feel rushed or forced into trades.

You always have something expiring—and something brewing.

7. Use the Average Premium Formula to Forecast Income

Over several weeks, your premiums will average out.

Example premiums:

- $95
- $110
- $105
- $100

Average = $102.50/week per position

Multiply by number of positions to project your monthly income with impressive accuracy.

Nugget: Income Becomes Predictable After 4–6 Weeks

When you average your premiums, volatility smooths out and your portfolio becomes stable and repeatable.

8. Avoid Income Targets During High-Volatility Events

Skip your targets when:

- Earnings are approaching
- Major economic events occur
- The market is panicking
- IV is unstable

Protecting your capital is more important than hitting a weekly number.

Nugget: Good Traders Skip Bad Weeks

Professionals know when *not* to trade, and that's why they stay in the game long enough to become profitable.

9. Income Targets Keep You Disciplined

When you have weekly goals, you avoid:

- Taking trades that don't fit the plan
- Panicking when a position goes red
- Deviating from delta rules
- Chasing risky premiums

Your system controls your behavior—not the market.

Nugget: Discipline Produces Income. Emotion Destroys It.

Targets don't just guide your choices…

they protect you from yourself.

In This Chapter, You Learned:

- Why income targets matter
- How to set realistic weekly numbers
- How many positions you need
- How to match premiums to targets
- How income cycles help planning
- Why chasing big premiums is dangerous
- How to forecast income
- Why discipline beats emotion

CHAPTER 16

TOOLS AND PLATFORMS

Professional results require professional tools.

The Wheel Strategy is simple, but running it consistently becomes easier—and more profitable—when you use platforms that provide accurate data, clean charts, and fast execution.

This chapter covers the best tools used by options traders today, what each one does, and how to integrate them into your income system.

1. Your Broker Is Your Foundation

A strong broker gives you:

- Reliable execution
- Good fills
- Clear option chains
- Reasonable commissions
- Fast support when needed

Top Brokers for Wheel Traders

- Charles Schwab (Thinkorswim integrated)
- TD Ameritrade (Thinkorswim)

- Tradier (great for active sellers)
- Fidelity (excellent reliability)
- Interactive Brokers (lowest commissions)

Choose based on:

- Comfort
- Ease of use
- Tools you value most

Nugget: Your Broker Determines Your Experience

A great strategy with a bad broker still produces bad results.

Execution quality alone can add or subtract *thousands* of dollars per year for active sellers.

2. Thinkorswim (TOS)

Thinkorswim is a favorite of professionals because it offers:

- Excellent charts
- Detailed option chains
- IV rank and volatility tools
- Probability calculators
- Delta and Greek data
- Paper trading mode
- Market scanning tools

If you only use one platform, Thinkorswim may be the best choice.

Nugget: TOS Is the Gold Standard for Analysis

Most professional educators, traders, and institutions rely on Thinkorswim because it packs every tool in one place—for free.

3. OptionStrat

OptionStrat is extremely helpful for Wheel traders.

It gives you:

- Visual profit/loss charts
- Clear break-even analysis
- Rolling calculators
- Probability estimates
- Volatility tools

It's one of the easiest ways to see the real risk and reward of a trade at a glance.

Nugget: OptionStrat Is the Best Sanity Check Tool

Before placing a trade, one glance at OptionStrat can confirm whether a setup is smart, dangerous, or needs a better strike.

4. Barchart.com

Barchart is great for:

- IV Rank
- Historical volatility
- Options volume and open interest
- Earnings dates
- Screeners and custom scans

It's a powerful tool for identifying high-premium opportunities.

Nugget: IV Rank Lives Here

Nearly every professional options seller checks IV Rank before choosing a trade…

And Barchart makes it instant, accurate, and free.

5. Yahoo Finance / TradingView / Finviz

These are fantastic for:

- Basic charts
- News
- Earnings calendar
- Fundamental data
- Support and resistance levels

TradingView

- Best charting tools
- Custom indicators
- Clean, easy interface

Finviz

- Best stock screener
- Filters for fundamentals and technicals

Yahoo Finance

- Simple and fast for quick research

Nugget: Use Simple Charting, Not Fancy Indicators

Wheel traders don't need complicated charts.

You're not predicting—you're preparing.

Clean charts = clean decisions.

6. Greeks and Probability Tools

Professional sellers rely on:

- Delta (probability of expiring ITM)
- Theta (time decay)
- IV (volatility)

The best tools for this are:

- Thinkorswim
- OptionStrat
- Barchart

You don't need advanced math—you just need accurate numbers.

Nugget: The Greeks Remove Emotion

When you know the probabilities, you stop guessing and start managing trades like a professional.

7. Spreadsheets and Trade Journals

Track your trades using:

- Excel
- Google Sheets
- Notion
- Apple Numbers

Your journal should include:

- Stock symbol
- Strike, premium, delta
- Entry and exit dates
- Rolling history
- Notes
- Outcome
- Weekly totals

Your journal becomes your blueprint for improvement.

Nugget: Journaling Creates Mastery

Almost every consistently profitable trader keeps detailed logs.

The masters don't rely on memory—they rely on records.

8. Charting Tools for the Wheel

You don't need complicated indicators.

Use:

- Basic trend lines
- Simple moving averages (SMA 20, SMA 50)
- Support and resistance zones

Your goal isn't to predict—it's to understand the environment.

Nugget: The Wheel Wins Without Prediction

You need to know:

- Is the stock stable?
- Trendy?
- Volatile?
- At support or resistance?

That alone gives you a major advantage.

9. Tools for Position Sizing

Use position calculators to determine:

- Safe allocation per trade
- Actual risk
- Break-even levels
- Percent returns

OptionStrat and TOS both offer excellent sizing tools.

Nugget: Bad Position Sizing Beats Good Strategy Every Time

Even the perfect strategy fails if your position is too big.

Sizing calculators prevent catastrophic overexposure.

10. Set and Review Tools

Many traders set alerts for:

- Price levels (support/resistance)
- Delta changes
- Premium levels
- Earnings dates

Thinkorswim and TradingView both have great alert systems.

Alerts help you manage trades without staring at the screen all day.

Nugget: Alerts Save You From Panic and FOMO

Instead of checking the market every 10 minutes, let your tools notify you only when action is needed.

This reduces emotional trading dramatically.

In This Chapter, You Learned:

- Which brokers are best for Wheel traders
- The power of Thinkorswim and OptionStrat
- Where to find IV Rank, charts, and earnings
- Why spreadsheets are essential
- How charting tools support better decisions
- How alerts help automate your system

CHAPTER 17

TAXES AND RECORDKEEPING

Selling options for income is a powerful strategy, but like any business, you must stay organized and understand how taxes apply to your profits.

The good news is this: options taxation in the US is straightforward, and with good recordkeeping, tax season becomes simple.

This chapter explains what you need to know (in plain English), how to stay organized, and how to treat your trading like a real income-producing business.

1. The Basics of Options Taxes

If you're trading in a taxable brokerage account, your option income is treated as:

- Short-term capital gains (ordinary income rate)
- Reported on your 1099-B at the end of the year

If you're trading in a Roth IRA or Traditional IRA:

- All option income grows tax-free (Roth)
- Or tax-deferred (Traditional IRA)
- No 1099-B reporting of gains each year

For many Wheel traders, IRAs are ideal for long-term compounding.

Nugget: The IRS Treats Option Premiums Like Any Other Income.

There are no hidden rules, no special forms, and no complex option-only tax structures.

If you can track premiums, you can handle taxes.

2. How Cash-Secured Puts Are Taxed

When you sell a put and it expires worthless, the premium is taxed as short-term gains.

You are assigned shares and:

- The premium reduces your cost basis on the shares.
- The assignment itself is *not* taxable.

Example:

- Sell $20 put for $1.00 premium
- Assigned at $20
- New cost basis = $19/share

This matters later if you sell the shares.

Nugget: Assignment Delays Taxes

When a put assigns, the premium doesn't show up as income—it quietly lowers your cost basis.

This is why assigned Wheel trades don't generate surprise tax bills.

3. How Covered Calls Are Taxed

When you sell a call, it expires worthless:

- Premium = short-term gain

You get assigned:

- Premium adjusts the sale price of the shares.
- This creates a capital gain or loss depending on your cost basis.

Example:

- Cost basis: $18
- Sell $20 call for $0.70
- Shares get called away at $20
- Sale price for tax purposes = $20.70

Nugget: Covered Calls Can Increase Your Share Sale Price

A called-away stock doesn't just sell at the strike…it sells at strike + premium, which sometimes turns a break-even trade into a strong profit on paper.

4. How Rolling Trades Are Taxed

When you roll a trade:

- You close one position
- You open another
- The first position triggers a realized gain or loss
- The new trade starts fresh

Rolling is *not* tax avoidance—it simply shifts gains/losses between trades.

Nugget: Rolls Create a Chain the IRS Doesn't See

Even though you see a rolling sequence, the IRS sees individual closed trades, each with their own gain or loss.

Rolls don't complicate your taxes—they simplify your book balance.

5. Tracking Your Trades

You *must* track:

- Date opened
- Date closed
- Premium received
- Premium paid (for closing/rolling)
- Strike prices

- Assignment dates
- New cost basis if assigned
- Notes

A good spreadsheet makes this simple.

Nugget: Tracking Prevents Phantom Gains

Without a journal, you forget premiums or miscount strikes, and you start thinking a trade is red when it's actually profitable.

6. Your Broker Tracks Everything

At the end of the year, your broker will send you:

- Form 1099-B
- A detailed list of every trade
- A record of all profits and losses
- Your total short-term gains

You (or your tax preparer) will input these into:

- Form 8949
- Schedule D

Most brokers allow automatic import into TurboTax or tax software.

Nugget: Your Broker Does 95% of the Work

All your spreadsheets and journals help *you,* but your broker's final documents are what the IRS cares about.

7. Why Recordkeeping Helps You Improve

Recordkeeping isn't just for taxes.

When you track consistently, you begin to see patterns:

- Which stocks perform best
- How much premium you earn weekly
- Which deltas work best

- How often you roll
- Why certain trades succeed or fail
- Whether your strikes are too aggressive
- Whether your position sizes are appropriate

Your journal becomes your edge.

Nugget: Your Data Is More Valuable Than Your Broker's Data.

Brokers tell you what happened.

Your journal tells you *why* it happened—and how to improve it.

8. Track Weekly Income Like a Business

Your log should show:

- Weekly premium totals
- Monthly totals
- Year-to-date revenue

This allows you to treat trading like a business with real revenue, real expenses, and real goals.

Wheel traders who treat trading like a business earn more and stress less.

Nugget: The Wheel Is a Business

Any activity with consistent income, measurable results, and repeatable processes is a business—and businesses thrive with good bookkeeping.

9. Consider a CPA If Your Account Is Large

A CPA can save you time and headaches once your account exceeds:

- $100,000+ in active trading
- *or* multiple Wheel positions weekly
- *or* if you run an LLC

Many traders also:

- Deduct trading-related expenses
- Deduct educational materials
- Deduct trading software
- Deduct home office expenses (if structured properly)

Talk to a CPA before taking deductions.

Nugget: A Good CPA Saves More Than They Cost

Most active traders who hire a CPA end up keeping more money after taxes *and* gain time back every month.

In This Chapter, You Learned:

- How options are taxed in cash accounts and IRAs
- How puts and calls affect cost basis
- How rolling creates realized gains/losses
- How to track everything properly
- How brokers simplify tax reporting
- How recordkeeping improves your system
- When to consider a CPA

CHAPTER 18

MINDSET OF A PROFESSIONAL OPTION SELLER

By now, you understand that selling options isn't just a financial strategy—it's a discipline.

Your mindset is the engine that keeps the Wheel turning, keeps your emotions in check, and keeps your trading consistent through good markets and bad.

This chapter brings together the mental frameworks used by top-tier option sellers so you can trade with confidence, clarity, and long-term focus.

1. Treat Trading Like a Business

Businesses don't:

- Panic
- Guess
- Chase
- Hope
- Go all-in

Businesses make decisions based on:

- Systems
- Probability
- Risk management
- Consistency

Your trading must operate the same way.

Every options seller is running a small business even if they trade from their phone.

Nugget: Businesses Thrive on Rules. Traders Fail Without Them.

A business with no structure collapses.

A trader with no system blows up.

Your rules *are* your protection.

2. You Are Not Predicting: You Are Managing Probability

Most traders ask:

- "Is the stock going to go up?"
- "Is the stock going to go down?"

Professional sellers ask:

- "What is the probability this trade succeeds?"
- "Is the premium worth the risk?"
- "Is this stock strong enough to run the Wheel on?"

You are not a fortune teller.

You are a probability manager.

Nugget: Your Job Is not *to Be Right*

Your Job Is to Be Prepared.

Prediction leads to ego.

Probability leads to income.

3. You Don't Need to Win Every Trade

Some trades will go red.

Some trades will need rolling.

Some trades will get assigned.

Some covered calls will be too aggressive.

Some puts will be tested.

This is normal.

Wheel traders win because:

- Premium lowers their cost basis
- They roll effectively
- They trade quality stocks
- They take profits early
- They never oversize positions

Winning every trade is not the goal—winning consistently is.

Nugget: A 70% Win Rate Can Beat a 100% Win Rate

The Wheel isn't about perfection.

It's about collecting premium, improving your position, and compounding long-term.

4. Patience Beats Intelligence

The Wheel rewards:

- Waiting for the right strike
- Letting theta decay work
- Giving your rolls time
- Letting winners finish
- Letting assignment happen when appropriate

The market pays patient traders far more than brilliant ones.

Nugget: Patience Prints Money

Time decay and rolling only work if you actually give them time to work.

Impatient traders donate to the market.

5. Emotional Control Is Your Edge

Your ability to stay calm directly determines your income.

When traders get emotional, they:

- Sell strikes that are too close
- Panic during red days
- Overtrade
- Break their rules
- Mismanage risk
- Blow up accounts

When you stay calm, you:

- Follow your system
- Stick to deltas
- Focus on probabilities
- Let time decay work
- Manage trades rationally

This is the professional advantage.

Nugget: Emotional Traders Make Bad Traders Rich

Every panic sale, every greedy strike, every oversized trade…

funds someone else's disciplined Wheel.

6. Consistency Over Excitement

Traders who seek excitement:

- Blow up accounts
- Jump into low-quality stocks

- Chase home run premiums
- Hold trades through earnings
- Trade too big

Professional sellers do the opposite:

- Sell safe strikes
- Choose stable companies
- Roll when appropriate
- Close early
- Trade the Wheel repeatedly
- Treat trading like a routine, not a thrill

Consistency beats excitement every time.

Nugget: Boring Traders Make the Most Money

If your trading is exciting, it's probably too risky.

The Wheel should feel calm and predictable.

7. Know Your Why

Your mindset becomes stronger when you know your purpose.

Ask yourself:

- Why am I trading options?
- What income am I seeking?
- What long-term freedom do I want?
- How will consistent premiums help my lifestyle?

Your purpose gives you discipline.

Nugget: Purpose Defeats Fear

When you know *why* you're trading, red days don't shake you—they strengthen your resolve.

8. The Wheel Is a Long-Term Wealth System

You're not trying to get rich overnight.

You're trying to build:

- Monthly income
- Lower cost basis
- Long-term share ownership
- A compounding machine
- A stress-free trading habit
- A scalable system

Every month you run the Wheel, your position improves.

Every year you run it, your portfolio becomes stronger.

You're building wealth, slowly, steadily, reliably.

Nugget: The Wheel Is a Marathon, Not a Sprint

Fast trading burns accounts.

Slow trading builds empires.

In This Chapter, You Learned:

- Trading is a business
- You manage probability, not predictions
- You don't need a 100% win rate
- Patience beats intelligence
- Emotional control is your real edge
- Consistency beats excitement
- Your why strengthens your discipline
- The Wheel is designed for long-term wealth building

Part V

CASE STUDIES AND TEMPLATES

CHAPTER 19

THE WHEEL IN ACTION USING HIMS STOCK

This chapter uses example prices for clarity. Real-world prices will vary. Always check the current option chain before placing trades.

Now it's time to take everything you've learned and see it applied in a real, step-by-step example.

For this case study, we'll use HIMS (Hims & Hers Health)—a stock that has become a favorite among Wheel traders because of:

- Strong fundamentals
- Steady growth
- High liquidity
- Consistent IV
- Attractive weekly premiums

This chapter will walk you through a full Wheel cycle using a realistic example based on a $39 current share price.

1. Why HIMS Is a Great Wheel Candidate

Before placing any trade, always ask, "Is this stock safe and predictable enough for the Wheel?"

HIMS is ideal because:

- It's not a meme stock
- It has real revenue growth
- Options are liquid with tight spreads
- Weekly expirations provide flexibility
- IV is consistently moderate to high
- The stock trades in clean, predictable ranges

This combination makes HIMS one of the most reliable Wheel stocks on the market.

Nugget: Your First Strike Choice Matters More Than You Think

Your very first put strike determines:

- Your future cost basis
- Your covered call choices
- Your assignment probability
- Your long-term profitability

A smart first strike sets up an easy Wheel cycle.

A greedy one creates stress later.

2. Step 1: Selling the First Cash-Secured Put

With HIMS trading at $39, a comfortable entry choice may be:

- **Strike:** $36 put
- **Delta:** ~0.22
- **Premium:** $0.70
- **Expiration:** 7 days

This means:

- You collect **$70** upfront
- You agree to buy 100 shares at $36
- Your break-even becomes **$35.30**

This is a textbook Wheel start.

3. Possible Outcomes of the First Put

Outcome A: Stock Stays Above $36

- Put expires worthless
- You keep the $70
- You sell another put next week

This is the smoothest scenario.

Outcome B: Stock Drops Below $36

You're assigned 100 shares at $36, but your real cost is $36 – $0.70 = $35.30 per share.

This sets you up perfectly for the covered call phase.

Nugget: Premiums Are Great, But Liquidity Is King

High premiums mean nothing if spreads are wide.

HIMS typically has tight spreads (often $0.05–$0.10), which dramatically improves execution quality.

4. Step 2: Selling the Covered Call

You now own 100 shares at a cost basis of $35.30.

Next step:

- Sell the $40 call
- Premium: $0.60
- Expiration: 7 days

You collect $60 instantly.

Your total premiums so far: $70 + $60 = $130

Your adjusted cost basis becomes: $35.30 – $0.60 = $34.70

5. Possible Outcomes of the Covered Call

Outcome A: Stock Stays Below $40

- Call expires worthless
- You keep the premium
- You still own your shares
- You sell another call next week

Perfect for long-term income.

Outcome B: Stock Rises Above $40

Your shares are called away at $40.

Your profit:

- Share gain = $40 – $35.30 = $4.70/share
- Premiums = $130

= $600 total profit for the cycle

Then you restart the Wheel by selling another put.

Nugget: Assignment Is Not a Punishment. It's Fuel.

Assignment on quality stocks is one of the most profitable parts of the Wheel.

It accelerates gains, reduces cost basis, and resets the cycle cleanly.

6. Step 3: The Wheel Repeats Automatically

Once your shares are called away:

- You hold cash again
- You keep all profits and premiums
- You restart the Wheel with another put

You might choose the $36 or $35 strike depending on IV and technicals that week.

7. What If HIMS Drops Hard?

If HIMS drops from $39 into a lower price range (for example $32–$34), you have options:

1. Accept Assignment

You're holding shares of a company you chose intentionally.

2. Roll the Put Out and Down

Example roll:

- Original strike: $36
- Roll to: $34
- Credit received: $0.40

New break-even:

- $35.30 (original)
- – $0.40 (roll credit)

= $34.90

3. Use Covered Calls to Repair Cost Basis

Selling calls at $36, $37, or $38 steadily reduces your break-even.

Nugget: Your Best Covered Calls Come from Calm Markets

Sideways price action allows covered calls to shine.

Theta burns fast, IV stabilizes, and call income becomes very consistent.

8. Long-Term Outcome: The Wheel Snowballs

After several cycles:

- Your cost basis drops repeatedly
- Premium income becomes predictable
- You learn the stock's behavior
- Your account grows steadily

- Your stress level falls
- Your trading confidence increases

This is how the Wheel compounds month after month.

Nugget: The Wheel Works Best on Stocks With Predictable Ranges

HIMS historically trades in well-defined channels.

Clear ranges allow you to confidently choose put and call strikes—one of the biggest advantages for Wheel traders.

9. Summary of the HIMS Wheel Cycle (Using $39 Price)

You collected:

- **$70** from the put
- **$60** from the call

= $130 total premium

Your effective cost basis became:

- $36 – $0.70 = $35.30
- $35.30 – $0.60 = $34.70

If your shares are eventually called away at $40:

- Share profit = $4.70/share = $470
- Premium = $130

= $600 total profit for the full Wheel cycle

This example illustrates a clean Wheel cycle.

In real trading, a full cycle usually unfolds over multiple weeks depending on market movement, volatility, and strike selection.

In This Chapter, You Learned:

- Why HIMS is a strong Wheel candidate
- How to choose smart strikes for puts and calls
- How assignment benefits the Wheel
- How rolling repairs positions
- How premium lowers cost basis
- Why predictable ranges and liquidity matter
- What a full, real-world Wheel cycle looks like

CHAPTER 20

AMD AND RGTI CASE STUDIES

To truly understand how flexible and powerful the Wheel Strategy is, it helps to see how it performs on two completely different stocks:

- AMD – large-cap, highly liquid, stable technology leader
- RGTI – A mid-cap, extremely high-volatility stock with explosive price swings

These two case studies show how the Wheel performs in both steady and wild market conditions, and how to adjust your approach accordingly.

Part 1: The AMD Wheel Cycle (Large-Cap, Stable Premiums—Using $217 Price)

Why AMD Makes a Great Wheel Candidate

AMD at $217 is:

- Highly liquid
- Volatile enough to produce strong weekly premiums
- Fundamentally solid
- Widely held by institutions
- Easy to roll due to tight spreads
- A stock that recovers quickly from dips

This makes AMD one of the best core Wheel stocks for building stable, predictable income.

Nugget: Large-Cap Stocks Reward Patience More Than Timing

You do not need perfect entries with AMD.

Consistency beats timing every single week.

1. Selling the First Cash-Secured Put on AMD

Assume AMD is trading at $217.00.

You choose:

- Strike: $207 put
- Delta: ~0.20
- Premium: $2.70
- Expiration: 7 days

You collect: $2.70 × 100 = $270

Break-even: $207 – $2.70 = $204.30

This is a safe, textbook Wheel entry with plenty of premium.

2. Outcomes of the AMD Put

Outcome A: AMD stays above $207

- The put expires worthless
- You keep $270
- You repeat the cycle next week

Outcome B: AMD dips slightly

- You get assigned at $207, but your real cost is: $204.30

Now you move to covered calls.

Nugget: Assignment on Strong Companies Is an Advantage

Wheel traders *want* assignment on quality names.

It's not a loss. You bought a great stock at a discount and were paid for it.

3. Running the Covered Call on AMD

Your cost basis = $204.30

You sell:

- $217 call
- Premium: $2.20
- Expiration: 7 days

You collect $220 instantly.

Total premium so far: $270 (put) + $220 (call) = $490

Your new cost basis becomes: $204.30 – $2.20 = $202.10

Beautiful improvement.

4. Possible Outcomes of the AMD Call

Outcome A: AMD stays below $217

- Call expires worthless
- You keep your shares
- You keep the premium
- You sell another call next week

Outcome B: AMD rises above $217

- Shares are called away
- Your profits: Your total profit comes from two sources—the gain on the shares when they are called away, plus the option premium you collected.
- Share gain: $217 – $204.30 = $12.70/share = $1,270
- Premiums collected: $490
- Total Wheel cycle profit: $1,760

Then you restart the Wheel with another put.

5. Why AMD Is a Great Wheel Stock at $217

- Excellent liquidity
- Tight bid/ask spreads
- Premiums scale well with price
- Easy to roll
- Assignments are profitable
- Predictable trading behavior

AMD belongs at the core of a stable Wheel portfolio.

Nugget: High-Priced Stocks Give Big Premiums but Demand Discipline

Large contracts = large dollar moves.

Position sizing is critical.

Never oversize a Wheel trade on expensive stocks.

Part 2: The RGTI Wheel Cycle (High Volatility, High Premiums—Using $28 Price)

RGTI at $28.00 behaves like a mid-cap, high-IV tech stock with explosive intraday movement:

- Larger premiums
- Fast reversals
- Frequent assignment
- Frequent rolling
- Big cost-basis improvement potential
- Higher risk

This is the fast-income part of your Wheel portfolio.

Nugget: High-IV Stocks Pay You More Because They Can Hurt You More

A $1.35 premium at a $25 strike is massive.

It exists because the stock can swing wildly.

This is opportunity *and* danger.

1. Selling the First Cash-Secured Put on RGTI

Assume RGTI is trading at $28.00.

You choose:

- Strike: $25 put
- Delta: ~0.25
- Premium: $1.35
- Expiration: 7 days

You collect: $135

Break-even: $25 – $1.35 = $23.65

This is an excellent return for a mid-cap high-volatility stock.

2. Outcomes of the RGTI Put

Outcome A: RGTI stays above $25

- Put expires worthless
- You keep $135
- Repeat the cycle next week

Outcome B: RGTI drops

- You are assigned at $25
- Your real cost basis is $23.65

Time to sell calls.

3. Running the Covered Call on RGTI

Sell:

- $28 call
- Premium: $1.10
- Expiration: 7 days

You collect: $110

Total premium so far: $135 + $110 = $245

New cost basis becomes: $23.65 – $1.10 = $22.55

Nugget: Small Caps Reward Active Traders, Not Passive Ones

RGTI requires:

- More monitoring
- More rolling
- Faster decisions
- Emotional discipline

This is not a set it and forget it stock.

4. Possible Outcomes of the RGTI Call

Outcome A: RGTI stays below $28

- Call expires worthless
- You keep shares
- You keep the premium
- You sell another call

You can realistically make $80–$120 premiums weekly in a high-IV environment.

Outcome B: RGTI rises above $28

- Shares get called away
- Share profit: $28 – $23.65 = $4.35/share = $435
- Premium profit: $245
- Total cycle profit: $680

This is a strong return from one high-IV cycle.

5. Why RGTI Is a High-Income Wheel Stock

- Huge premiums
- Big extrinsic value, perfect for sellers
- Fast cost-basis improvement
- Rolling is easy because IV stays high

But watch out for:

- Sharp pullbacks
- Emotional trading
- Oversizing
- Violent price swings
- Frequent adjustments

This stock belongs in your high-income segment, not your foundation.

Nugget: Use High-IV Stocks for Income, Not Long-Term Ownership

You run the Wheel on stocks like RGTI to extract premium, not to invest for decades.

AMD vs. RGTI: A Direct Comparison (Using Updated Prices)

Category	AMD ($217)	RGTI ($28)
Stock Type	Large-cap, stable	Mid-cap, explosive volatility
Premiums	Moderate to strong	Very high
IV	Medium	Extremely high
Assignment Risk	Low	High
Wheel Cycles	Smooth, consistent	Fast-paced, jumpy
Rolling	Occasional	Frequent
Ideal For	Stability, foundation	High-income, high-IV segment

Both stocks absolutely have value but for very different roles in your Wheel portfolio.

- How the Wheel performs on a stable large-cap (AMD @ $217)
- How the Wheel performs on a volatile mid-cap (RGTI @ $28)
- How volatility affects premiums, rolls, and risk
- How cost basis steadily improves through premium selling
- How to mix stable and high-IV stocks for balanced income

CHAPTER 21

TEMPLATES AND TRACKERS

The best traders don't just place trades—they track, measure, and review them.

Tracking transforms selling options from a hobby into a predictable income system.

These tools help you:

- Stay disciplined
- Avoid emotional trades
- Spot mistakes early
- Measure performance
- Build consistency

1. Weekly Options Income Tracker

Weekly Options Tracker Template

Week of: ________________________

Ticker	Strategy	Strike	Exp. Date	Delta	Premium In	Premium Out	Net Income	Notes
	CSP/CC							
	CSP/CC							
	CSP/CC							

Total Premium This Week: $________________

Nugget of Wisdom #1: If You Don't Track It, You Can't Improve It.

Professionals treat tracking as data collection, not busywork.

2. Monthly Options Income Summary

Monthly Summary Template

Month: ______________________________

Week   Total Premium Notes

Week 1 $______________________________

Week 2 $______________________________

Week 3 $______________________________

Week 4 $______________________________

Week 5 $______________________________

Monthly Total: $__________________

Monthly Goal: $__________________

Difference: $____________________

Nugget: Consistency Creates Predictability, and Predictability Creates Confidence.

Tracking month-to-month reveals:

- Patterns
- Seasonal volatility
- Premium cycles
- Your personal strengths

3. Wheel Strategy Position Tracker

Wheel Position Template

Ticker: ________________________

Starting Date: ____________________

Step	Action	Strike	Premium	Cost Basis Impact	Notes
1	Sell Put			Lowers cost basis	
2	Roll Put			Adds credit / safer strike	
3	Assigned Shares			Sets share cost	
4	Sell Covered Call			Lowers cost basis	
5	Roll Call			Raises strikeextends time	
6	Shares Called Away			Record profit	

Final Profit for the Cycle: $__________________

Nugget: The Wheel Isn't Guesswork—It's a Documented Machine.

When every step is recorded, the strategy becomes repeatable and scalable.

4. Cost Basis Calculator

Cost Basis Record

Item	Amount
Original Strike	__________
Original Premium	__________
Roll Credits	__________
Covered Call Premiums	__________
Total Premium Collected	__________
True Cost Basis = Strike – Total Premium	

Final Cost Basis Per Share: $__________________

Nugget: Your Real Profit Is Hidden in the Cost Basis, Not the Chart.

Charts show noise.

Cost basis shows truth.

5. Pre-Trade Checklist (Professional Version)

Pre-Trade Checklist

- Is the stock fundamentally strong?
- Is IV high enough?
- Is delta between 0.15–0.30?
- Am I willing to own the shares?
- Is the position size safe?
- Are earnings far enough away?
- Do I have a plan if it drops?
- Do I have a plan if it spikes?
- Does this trade help me hit my weekly goals?

Nugget: Amateurs React. Professionals Prepare.

A checklist removes emotion and replaces it with process.

6. Rolling Decision Flowchart

Rolling Flowchart

Is the option ITM?

- No → Hold or close at 50%

- Yes → Continue ↓

Is the stock fundamentally strong?

- No → Close or accept assignment

- Yes → Continue ↓

Can I roll for credit?

- Yes → Roll out/down

- No → Roll for probability or accept assignment

Nugget: Rolling Isn't Emotional—It's Engineering.

Rolling lets you remodel the trade into something safer and more profitable.

7. Long-Term Income Projection Sheet

Projection Template

Average Premium Per Position: $____________

Number of Wheel Positions: ______________

Timeframe	Projected Income
Monthly	$__________________
Quarterly	$__________________
Yearly	$__________________

Nugget: When You Know Your Numbers, You Control Your Trading—Not the Market.

Forecasting transforms your portfolio into a predictable income engine.

In This Chapter, You Learned:

- How to track weekly and monthly results
- How to document each Wheel cycle
- How to calculate true cost basis
- How to use checklists to prevent mistakes
- How to build rolling rules into your process
- How to forecast income like a business
- Why Nuggets sharpen your discipline and mindset

CHAPTER 22

COMPOUNDING AND SCALING THE WHEEL

The real power of selling options doesn't come from one trade, one cycle, or even one month of premiums. It comes from time, repetition, and scaling—the same forces that build wealth in every successful business.

This chapter shows you how to grow your Wheel Strategy from a single position into a true income engine, and how compounding transforms small, steady premiums into long-term financial freedom.

1. The Wheel Is Designed for Compounding

Every time you:

- Sell a put
- Sell a call
- Roll for credit
- Lower your cost basis
- Increase your probability
- Repeat the cycle

…your portfolio becomes stronger.

Your income grows because your cost basis drops week after week, month after month, year after year.

This is compounding in action.

Nugget: Professionals Build Wealth by Pennies, Not by Windfalls

Most premium gains are small, but repeated hundreds of times per year.

The Wheel compounds faster than dividend investing because you are lowering cost basis continuously.

2. Reinvest Premiums Into New Wheel Positions

The simplest and most powerful way to scale is to use your premium income to fund additional Wheel positions.

Example:

- You earn $400 in premiums this month
- You add that cash to your account
- Next month, you sell a second put
- Your income doubles

That second Wheel then creates enough income to fund a third.

By the time you're running 3–5 Wheels, your account becomes self-sustaining.

Nugget: The Fastest Scaling Happens From Wheel #2 to Wheel #3

Once two Wheels are running, the third can often be funded entirely by premium income, not outside deposits.

This is the point where the account begins to grow itself.

3. Scaling Position Size Gradually

Never jump from:

- 1 contract → 10

or

- $2,000 positions → $20,000 positions

Instead, scale like a professional:

- Increase by 1 contract at a time
- Or increase allocation by 10–20%
- Only scale when you feel zero emotional stress

If the position size makes you nervous, it's too big.

Nugget: Your Stress Level Is a Position Sizing Indicator

If you feel anxiety watching the position, the size is incorrect.

Professionals size positions based on emotional control, not greed.

4. Diversify Across Different Wheel Types

Scaling safely means diversifying into:

A. Low-IV Stable Wheel Stocks

KO, WMT, INTC, PEP

→ steady but smaller premiums

B. Moderate-IV Growth Stocks

AMD, HIMS, PLTR

→ ideal balance of risk and income

C. High-IV High-Yield Stocks

RGTI, MARA, RIVN

→ massive premiums, higher risk

Diversification smooths income and reduces stress.

Nugget: High IV Should Rarely Exceed 10% of Portfolio Size

High-IV tickers like RGTI generate huge returns, but keeping allocation small protects your account during volatility spikes.

5. Stagger Your Expirations

Instead of having everything expire the same Friday, stagger expirations at:

- 7-days
- 14-days
- 30-days

This creates:

- Weekly income
- Monthly income
- Constant rolling opportunities

Nugget: Staggered Expirations Reduce Stress Better Than Any Other Scaling Technique

Not having all trades expiring the same day lowers emotional pressure and increases flexibility.

6. Use Rolling to Extend Your Income Stream

Rolling correctly:

- Lowers cost basis
- Increases probability
- Extends time
- Generates more credit
- Stabilizes the position

Rolling is how professionals turn losing setups into long-term winners.

Nugget: Rolling Is Income Refinancing

Think about rolling like refinancing a loan except you get paid to extend the terms.

Rolls extend income and reduce risk at the same time.

7. Avoid Overscaling During High Volatility

Do *not* scale up during:

- Market crashes
- Sudden IV spikes
- Earnings season
- Major news events

During high volatility:

- Reduce size
- Choose safer strikes
- Prioritize cash

Nugget: Most Wheel Failures Occur from Scaling During IV Spikes

IV spikes inflate premiums *and* risk.

Scale only during calm periods, not storms.

8. The Snowball Effect of Long-Term Wheel Trading

After 1 year:

- Income improves
- Strikes become safer
- Rolling becomes intuitive

After 2 years:

- 50–70% of your portfolio may run the Wheel
- Premium income becomes predictable

After 5 years:

- The Wheel becomes a wealth-building engine
- You grow even if withdrawing income

Nugget: The Wheel Outperforms Dividend Investing Over Time

Because dividends pay quarterly…

But option premiums pay weekly, bi-weekly, or monthly and compound instantly.

9. Track Your Scaling Progress

Scaling Log

Date	# of Wheel Positions	Avg Premium	Total Weekly Income	Notes

Tracking creates visibility and motivation.

Nugget: Traders Who Track Income Grow Accounts 2–3× Faster

Data creates discipline.

Discipline creates consistency.

Consistency creates profit.

10. Scaling Safely Turns You Into a Professional

Professionals:

- Scale slowly
- Diversify across volatility levels
- Maintain small high-IV exposure
- Reinvest premiums
- Let compounding do the work

Success isn't about one big trade.

It's about hundreds of small victories.

In This Chapter, You Learned:

- How compounding strengthens the Wheel
- How reinvesting premiums accelerates growth
- How to scale positions safely
- How to diversify Wheel categories
- How staggered expirations create stability
- How rolling protects positions
- How to avoid dangerous scaling
- How long-term repetition builds wealth

CHAPTER 23

AVOIDING COMMON MISTAKES OF NEW OPTION SELLERS

Even with a simple, disciplined strategy like the Wheel, beginners often fall into predictable traps.

The good news?

Every one of these mistakes is avoidable once you know what to look out for.

This chapter highlights the most common errors new traders make, why they happen, and how *you* can prevent them from ever impacting your portfolio.

1. Chasing High Premiums

This is the #1 beginner mistake.

A new trader sees a put offering huge premium and thinks, *Wow, that's easy money!*

But high premiums almost always mean:

- Extremely high volatility
- High risk of assignment

- High chance the stock collapses
- Emotional stress
- Hard-to-manage rolls

Professionals avoid chasing premium. They choose probability over excitement.

Nugget: High Premium = High Risk

When a premium looks too good to be true, it usually comes with risk you haven't seen yet.

2. Selling Options on Bad Stocks

Many beginners sell puts on cheap stocks because they seem less risky.

But cheap stocks are often cheap for a reason:

- Weak fundamentals
- No revenue
- High dilution
- Pending bankruptcy risk
- Wild volatility

This destroys Wheel cycles.

This is why your foundation must always be to only sell options on stocks you're willing to own.

This rule alone will save your portfolio.

3. Oversizing Your Trades

The second-biggest mistake:

Putting too much of your account into one position.

If the stock moves against you, you can't:

- Roll easily
- Manage the assignment
- Control the risk
- Stay calm emotionally

Professional rule:

No more than 20% of your account in *any* single Wheel position.

4. Rolling Too Late

Beginners wait until:

- The option is deep ITM
- There's almost no extrinsic value left
- The roll becomes expensive

Pros roll early, while there is still:

- High IV
- Extrinsic value
- Time
- Flexibility

Rolling early keeps you in control.

5. Selling Covered Calls Too Close to the Money

This happens when beginners want:

- More premium
- Faster money
- Safe enough setups

But selling calls too close to the money leads to:

- Losing your shares prematurely
- Poor strike selection
- Lower overall profits

Professionals choose strikes that balance:

- Income
- Distance
- Probability

Not greed.

6. Ignoring Earnings Dates

Earnings can wreck a perfectly good Wheel position.

New traders often forget to check earnings week, leading to:

- Huge volatility
- Bad assignment
- Hard-to-manage rolls
- Unexpected losses

Professional rule:

If the trade you're about to sell includes an upcoming earnings announcement in its expiration window, skip the trade and wait until after earnings to sell. Earnings introduce unpredictable volatility and unnecessary risk.

In This Chapter, You Learned:

- Why chasing big premiums causes big losses
- Which stocks to avoid for the Wheel
- Why position sizing keeps you safe
- Why rolling early protects you
- How covered call distance affects profit
- Why earnings must *always* be checked

CHAPTER 24

FINAL THOUGHTS: BECOMING THE TRADER YOU WERE MEANT TO BE

You've reached the end of this book, but your journey as a trader is just beginning.

If you apply what you learned with discipline, patience, and consistency, you can generate steady income, protect your capital, and grow your wealth over time.

The Wheel Strategy isn't about thrills.

It's about freedom.

Freedom from guessing.

Freedom from stress.

Freedom from hoping the market will be kind to you.

With the Wheel, you create your own paycheck.

1. Your Success Will Come From Repetition

Each week that you:

- Sell a put
- Sell a call
- Roll for credit
- Track your trades
- Improve your discipline

…you become a stronger trader.

You don't need brilliance, just consistency.

Nugget: Mastery Is Built Through Boring Repetition

If you want excitement, go skydiving.

If you want wealth, run the Wheel.

2. Keep Your System Simple

Simplicity wins.

Avoid:

- Overthinking
- Overtrading
- Exotic strategies
- Emotional trades
- Market predictions

Your three tools:

- Cash-secured puts
- Covered calls
- Rolling

…are more than enough to build financial freedom.

3. Protect Your Capital Above Everything Else

You can't generate income if you lose your capital.

Professionals focus on:

- Small, controlled risks
- Careful strike selection
- Reasonable position sizes
- Patience
- Consistency

Capital protection *is* the strategy.

4. Stay Patient, the Wheel Rewards Time

Some cycles will be fast.

Some cycles will be slow.

Some will require rolling.

Some will be perfect from start to finish.

But every cycle moves you forward.

Even losing trades teach you more than winning ones.

Nugget: Time + Discipline = Freedom

No one trade will change your life…

…but thousands of disciplined trades will.

5. You Now Have a Complete, Lifelong System

You learned something many traders never discover:

- How to create your own paycheck
- How to use probability instead of prediction
- How to lower your cost basis over time
- How to grow your account safely
- How to treat trading like a business

- How to stay emotionally centered
- How to reinvest premiums to scale

This is your system now.

In This Chapter, You Learned:

- Why repetition creates mastery
- Why simplicity beats complexity
- Why capital protection is your foundation
- Why patience builds wealth
- How the Wheel becomes a lifelong system

GLOSSARY (A–Z)

This glossary gives you fast, plain English definitions of every important options-trading term used throughout the book.

A

Adjustment: Any action you take to improve a position (rolling, closing, changing strikes).

Assignment: When the option buyer exercises the contract and you must buy/sell shares.

ATM (At the Money): A strike price very close to the current share price.

B

Bid/Ask Spread: The difference between the buying price (bid) and selling price (ask).

Break-Even Price: Strike price minus all premium collected (for puts) or cost basis plus premium (for calls).

Broker: The platform you trade through (Schwab, TOS, Fidelity, etc.).

C

Call Option: Gives someone the right to buy shares from you at the strike price.

Cash-Secured Put (CSP): A put you sell while holding enough cash to buy 100 shares.

Collateral: The cash or shares backing an option you sold.

Contract: One options contract controls 100 shares.

Cost Basis: The effective price you paid for the shares after premiums.

D

Debit: An amount you pay when entering or rolling a trade.

Delta: A Greek that approximates the probability of finishing ITM.

Dividends: Payments issued by some companies to shareholders.

E

Earnings: A company's quarterly financial announcement; premiums spike during this time.

Extrinsic Value: The time value of an option; what decreases each day due to theta.

Ex-Dividend Date: The cutoff date to receive dividends; can trigger early assignment of covered calls.

F

Fill: When your order executes.

Front-Month Options: The nearest expiration date.

G

Gamma: A Greek that measures how quickly delta changes.

Good 'Til Canceled (GTC): An order type that stays open until filled or canceled.

H

Hedge: A strategy to reduce risk.

High-IV Stock: A stock with high implied volatility and high premiums.

I

Implied Volatility (IV): The market's expectation of future price movement; affects premium.

In the Money (ITM): A strike that has intrinsic value.

Intrinsic Value: The real, immediate value of an option if exercised.

J

Journal: Your trading log where you track each trade, result, and note.

K

Key Support/Resistance: Price levels where stocks tend to bounce or stall.

L

Leverage: Using borrowed money or margin (not needed for the Wheel).

Liquidity: How easily you can enter or exit a trade with tight spreads.

M

Margin: Borrowed funds used in some option strategies (we use cash-secured trades).

Max Profit: The most you can earn on an options trade (usually the premium).

Max Loss: The worst-case scenario on a trade (rare with the Wheel).

Multi-Leg Strategy: Any options trade with more than one contract (spread, condor, etc.).

N

Net Credit: Total premium collected after selling an option or rolling a trade.

Net Debit: Total cost if you pay to adjust or buy back a position.

O

Open Interest (OI): The number of active option contracts at a given strike.

OTM (Out of the Money): A strike safely outside the stock price (Wheel traders love these).

Option Chain: The full list of all available strikes and expirations.

P

Premium: The money you collect when selling an option.

Probability of Profit (POP): The chance your trade expires out of the money.

Put Option: Gives someone the right to sell shares to you at the strike price.

P/L (Profit & Loss): Shows the change in value of your trade.

Q

Quantitative Analysis: Using data and metrics to evaluate trades.

Quote: The current bid/ask price for an option.

R

Risk-to-Reward: The relationship between potential loss and potential gain.

Roll: Closing one option and opening another to improve your position.

S

Short Option: An option you sold; you are collecting premium.

Spread: A multi-leg trade with one long and one short option.

Strike Price: Where shares will be bought/sold if assigned.

Support/Resistance: Areas where the stock historically reverses direction.

T

Theta: Measures daily time decay—the seller's biggest advantage.

Time Decay: The natural loss of extrinsic value as expiration approaches.

Thinkorswim (TOS): A popular trading platform for options sellers.

True Cost Basis: Strike minus all collected premiums (puts) or cost basis minus CC premiums.

U

Underlying Stock: The stock the option contract is based on.

V

Volatility: How fast or unpredictably a stock moves.

Vertical Spread: A defined-risk multi-leg trading strategy.

Vega: A Greek measuring how sensitive an option is to changes in IV.

Volatility Crush: Rapid drop in IV after earnings or major news—great for sellers.

W

Wheel Strategy: CSPs → Assignment → Covered Calls → Repeat.

Weekly Options: Options that expire every Friday (sometimes Tues/Thurs).

X

Expiration Cycle: The timeline of when options expire.

Y

Yield: Return on capital based on premium collected.

Z

Zero-DTE: Zero days to expiration (same-day options); not used in the Wheel.

CLOSING REFLECTIONS

Selling options is one of the most consistent and repeatable ways to generate income in the stock market. It doesn't require predicting the future, day-trading, perfect timing, or being smarter than everyone else.

It requires:

- Discipline
- Patience
- Consistency

As you follow the Wheel Strategy, selling cash-secured puts, accepting assignment when appropriate, selling covered calls, rolling when needed, and repeating the cycle, something shifts:

Your account becomes calmer. Your income steadier. Your stress lower. Your confidence higher. Your future clearer.

Most traders never experience this because they chase excitement instead of consistency.

But you're now different. You understand…

- the mechanics
- the psychology
- the probabilities
- the long-term strategy
- the compounding effect

…that make the Wheel a true wealth-building system.

You now trade with clarity, not fear. With process, not panic. With confidence, not confusion. Because you're not guessing—you're running a system.

If you stay committed, your financial future will be shaped by your decisions, not the randomness of the market.

To your consistent premiums…

To your growing account…

To your financial independence…

One option contract at a time.

ACKNOWLEDGMENTS

Writing this book has been a journey built on years of experience, countless trades, and a deep passion for helping others understand the power of selling options.

To my family—thank you for your patience, encouragement, and support.

To fellow traders and friends—thank you for the conversations, insights, and shared learning moments.

To early readers and those who provided feedback—your input strengthened this book.

To all readers—thank you for choosing this guide and investing in your own financial independence.

And finally, to the markets—unpredictable, unforgiving, and endlessly fascinating—the greatest teacher of all.

FEBRUARY 4, 2026
NYSE OPENING BELL®
LISTED
NEW YORK STOCK EXCHANGE
LISTED
NEW YORK STOCK EXCHANGE

ABOUT THE AUTHOR

Tony Perez is a multifaceted creator, trader, and storyteller whose work bridges financial strategy and military action fiction. As a self-taught trader, Tony is known for breaking down complex concepts into simple, actionable steps anyone can understand.

He emphasizes discipline over prediction and consistency over excitement, principles that form the backbone of this guide.

Tony is also the author of the James Chase military thriller series:

- *The Delta Mission*
- *The Dragon and the Eagle*
- *Cuba Libre*

Whether writing about battlefield strategy or financial strategy, Tony brings the same commitment: make it real, make it clear, and make it useful.

He lives in Florida, where he continues to trade, write, and help others build financial and personal freedom one mission and one premium at a time.

9 781735 523668